W9-BML-010

The History and Devotion of the Rosary

Richard Gribble, C.S.C.

Our Sunday Visitor Publishing Division
Our Sunday Visitor, Inc.
Huntington, Indiana 46750

Imprimi Potest: Carl F. Ebey, C.S.C.
Provincial Superior, Indiana Province
Congregation of Holy Cross
November 27, 1991

Nihil Obstat: Rev. John S. Dunne, C.S.C.
Censor Deputatus

ISBN: 0-87973-521-X
LCCCN: 92-80495

PRINTED IN THE UNITED STATES OF AMERICA

Cover design by Monica Watts.

521

This book is dedicated to my parents, Richard and Dorothy, from whom the seeds of faith were obtained and nurtured, to a long forgotten convert who introduced me to Fatima and the rosary, and to a good friend, Mary, who encouraged and challenged me to write these words.

Table of Contents

Foreword

I'm honored and privileged to be asked to write the foreword to the book, *The History and Devotion of the Rosary* by Richard Gribble, C.S.C.

In the early years of the Family Rosary Crusade, I had hoped that I could get thorough research done as to the origin, growth and development of the traditional rosary as we pray it today. Little did I think that it would be a brother priest in the Congregation of Holy Cross who would make available to the church and the world such a treasure. Better still that he would be one of our younger priests ordained in April 1989.

My words of praise and tribute are not adequate to express what Father Gribble's book means to me. It reflects the scholarship of its author. The extraordinary time he must have put into its making and best of all his belief in the power and efficacy of the rosary for "A greater understanding of the mystery of Christ celebrated within family prayer." "To Christians the rosary is vastly more than a means of counting prayer. It is a tradition-distilled essence of Christian devotion in which vocal and mental prayer unite the whole person in effective and purposeful meditation on the central mysteries of Christian belief. The rosary thus joins the human race to God through Mary whom God chose from all times for the specific purpose of Mother and intercessor." (Quotations from Father Gribble's book.)

May it be that Our Lord has chosen Father Gribble to be numbered as a member of the team that will bring the message, mission and ministry of the Family Rosary into the next century and beyond.

— Father Patrick Peyton, C.S.C.
(1909 - 1992)

[The author describes Father Peyton's role in encouraging use of the rosary. See Chapter 5.]

Preface

The rosary is a complete and most satisfying form of Christian prayer and devotion. Although at present the rosary seems to be suffering from an eclipse in popularity, its merit, worthiness and necessity continue to be proclaimed through the documents of Vatican II and the writings and proclamations of numerous organizations of bishops including the United States National Conference of Catholic Bishops. For centuries the simplicity, profundity, beauty and power of the rosary has been sung by saints, popes and many masters of the spiritual life. For many Roman Catholics the rosary has been a primer of the faith in which the basic Christian truths of the relationship between God and the human race are revealed. It is a staple of prayer, the daily bread of devotion, on which many of the faithful nourish their spiritual natures, as priests and religious additionally do with the Divine Office.

This book is my endeavor to gather together the historical origins of this most profound prayer form. Although apocryphal stories continue to be popular concerning the rosary, it is evident that its origins are not from the hand of our Blessed Mother to St. Dominic. Rather, the origins of the rosary consist of an evolutionary process which only in the last 200 to 250 years has taken the form we know today.

This book concentrates on the origin and development of this Christian prayer, yet many similar devices used for the counting of prayers are and have been used by many of the great religions of human history. The rosary, therefore, did not evolve of its own nature, but rather, as a counting form, can be traced to the period before the time of Christ.

This book attempts to give some idea of contemporary thought and theology concerning the rosary based on its Christian roots. Through the writings of such men as Pope Leo XIII and the work of Father Patrick Peyton, the rosary reached its height of popularity within our own century. The rosary is alive and still serves as a powerful companion in prayer for the faithful. A reawakening to the historicity and purpose of this prayer can bring people closer to God through the common Christian vocation to holiness and prayer.

— Richard Gribble, C.S.C.

Introduction

The Rosary: Facts and Legends

A rather simple yet feeble story tells of a priest exhorting young girls in imitating the Virgin Mary by picturing our Lady at the moment of the Annunciation: "What do you think Mary was doing when the angel Gabriel appeared to her? Was she cleaning house, gossiping with neighbors or reading? No! What else would she be doing but sitting quietly in her room saying her beads."[1]

The picture that one derives from this story makes it appear that the rosary has always been with us. Throughout many Christian centuries the rosary has found sufficient honor and tribute to establish it as a fixture within the spiritual practice of most Roman Catholics. Besides the apocryphal oration above, there have been serious attempts to trace the rosary, because of its status, back to Mary herself. Father Theophilus Raynaud actually wrote that the rosary was instituted by our Blessed Mother.[2] His proof for such a statement was to be found in the rosary beads left behind by Mary at her Assumption (the Dormitian), beads preserved in the Church of St. Maria in Campitelli in Rome. The relic, according to Herbert Thurston, S.J., "seems to have unduly provoked the derision of scoffers, and it is now no longer exhibited for veneration."[3]

Recognition of Mary as the principal source for the rosary has been defended by such notables as Prosper Lambertini, the future Pope Benedict XIV. Although the meaning is debatable, the Pope's words written in *Analecta Juris Pontificii* (1757) certainly come close to proposing a teaching on the subject: "The rosary could have been said by the Most Blessed Virgin Mary . . . but this does not imply that the Most Blessed Virgin Mary could have said the angelical salutation to reveal the mystery which that salutation accomplished."[4]

One feels safe in putting aside such isolated instances as devotional flights of fantasy brought forth to show the relationship between Mary and the prayer beads. There is nothing intrinsically impossible in viewing Mary with beads in her hands since use of such a device to count prayers is older than Christianity. But the considerations of what Mary might have been doing with a set of counter beads in her hands takes us away from our central task of tracing the historical development of the rosary as we know it today.

In the research conducted for this book, two basic hypotheses for the origin of the Christian rosary were analyzed. The first view, taken from a theory proposed by the "development of religion" advocates, states that the Christian rosary is derived from the prayer counters of Eastern religions. The second theory comes from the long unquestioned tradition that the rosary came to us essentially complete from the hands of St. Dominic. Both theories today have widespread appeal for many people.

Supporting the development of religion theory is the fact that Hindus and Buddhists have used prayer beads as measures for counting since before Christ. Muslims too have used beads for prayer counting since the seventh century. There is, however, no demonstrable fact which links the beads of Eastern religions with those of Christianity. Using some method to count long repetitions of prayer seems natural; there seems to be a separate spontaneous origin for prayer counters in many religious persuasions that historians have difficulty in tracing. When Sir Monier-Williams, a scholar in Indian society and religion, investigated the beginnings of Hindu prayer beads, he ultimately wrote that the questions of origins and priority of the rosary are insoluble with the means at our command.[5]

Historians of Muhammadan practice encounter a similar problem when investigating the origin of prayer beads. It appears that the first references to prayer counters are found at a time when similar development is seen in Christian practices. Spontaneity of the practice is thus evident. Tradition says that the prophet Muhammad chided some women for using pebbles to count their prayers, telling them to use their fingers. In contrast, however, Dr. Ignaz Goldhizer in the *Revue de l' Histoire des Religions* found that any documentary evidence for methods of counting prayers was highly doubtful until long after the death of Muhammad.[6]

Doctor Goldhizer's study does establish some dates for a natural development of the prayer counters in Islam. In a rebuke administered by Caliph Al-Hadi (C.E. 786) to his mother, Chezuma, when she tried to tell him how to govern the people, he stated, "It is not a woman's business to meddle in matters of state; get thee back to thy prayers and thy beads (subha)."[7] A second incident, dating circa 913, seems to indicate that beads were still a novelty. Abu-el-Kasim was reproached for using the beads and replied, "I cannot give up any practice that helps me draw nearer to God."[8] The usefulness of this analysis of Islamic practice is that simultaneous development of prayer beads in several of the world's great religions is certainly possible. Furthermore, the hypothesis that the Christian rosary evolved from Eastern religions is really not supportable.

Another popular theory connecting East and West is that the prayer beads were brought to Europe by Crusaders returning from the Holy Land. Although the work of Dr. Goldhizer shows that the prayer beads were most probably present in Islam during the period of the Crusades, the hypothesis that Crusaders introduced the rosary to the West seems to be based more on conjecture than fact. It is certainly not impossible that popular use of the beads was encouraged by such contact, yet this does not in any way detract from our theory of the separate development of the beads among Christians.

The tradition that Mary gave the beads to St. Dominic in the thirteenth century is worthy of investigation as well. This tradition is very strong in Roman Catholic circles and was not questioned for hundreds of years. The basic facts, however, give no justification to such a tradition. It is known that more than 200 years after St. Dominic's death, Blessed Alanus de Rupe wrote an account of a vision in which the Blessed Virgin Mary appeared to Dominic, revealing to him the devotion to the rosary and entrusting him with the task of promulgating its use.[9] This account quickly became fixed in the rosary tradition. Many statements, including some from the See of Peter, assume the Dominican connection with the rosary in their espousal of its benefits for the faithful. Additionally, artists multiplied representations of our Lady giving the beads to the saint. The story thus became firmly fixed in Christian thought and literature.

It was not until the mid-eighteenth century that anyone thought to examine the connection of the rosary to St. Dominic. In their painstaking separation of fact from fiction in the lives of the saints, the Bollandists (a group of Dutch Jesuits) could find no evidence that would link the origins of the rosary to Dominic. Nevertheless, despite the historical investigation of St. Dominic in *Acta Sanctorum* (published at Antwerp in 1733),[10] the spread of the tradition continued unabated. Five popes after this period credited St. Dominic with founding the rosary devotion.[11]

Not until the beginning of our century did the current hypothesis of an evolutionary development for the rosary come into common Christian understanding. The road was certainly not easy. In a series of articles on popular Christian devotions, Father Herbert Thurston, S.J., began to treat the rosary and its origins. Taking his lead from the work of the Bollandists, Thurston searched the medieval records for anything that could substantiate or refute the established tradition about St. Dominic and the rosary. He came to the conclusion that he could not connect any single feature in the past history of this devotion with the person of the founder of the Friars Preachers.[12] Father Thurston's articles had wide circulation and created quite a stir within the Roman Catholic world. Books and articles began to pour off the presses against the man who would challenge such a hallowed tradition. One (French) author expressly stated in the title of his article that it was a defense of the rosary tradition against Father Thurston.[13] Thus the harmless articles written by the learned Jesuit became dominated by controversy and threw Dominican scholarship into a tailspin.

Even if the tradition is not factually true, it is still perfectly valid to keep as legend. It is historical fact that St. Dominic had great devotion to our Lady and that he instilled that same devotion into the men and women who followed his way of life. The Dominicans are responsible for popularizing the rosary tradition, making it universal throughout the Church. All of the truths of which the rosary speaks are compressed and made concrete for us in the story of Mary's appearance to Dominic. The legend, therefore, is valid and useful. It must be remembered, however, that one should understand the vision as legend and not confuse it with historical fact. The correct attitude about the controversy is not one of contention. Rather, as a Dominican priest once told me, "It is not important to know the origins of the rosary; it is important, however, that one know how to pray it well."[14]

When we turn to reviewing the facts of the rosary's historical development, we find that the prayer is really the result of the people's desire to participate in Christian worship. This is especially true when one considers that during medieval times few people, other than religious and clerics, could either read or write Latin. Participation in the Mass and Divine Office was, therefore, severely restricted. We find, strange as it might seem, that Christian rosary beads are older than the Hail Mary. Additionally, rosaries of prayers and rosaries of mysteries grew up independently, then joined together.

The origins of the rosary and how it won universal acceptance has not been definitely traced in all its detail. We do have, however, a mass of historical data from which emerges the general historical development outlined in the following pages. The evolutionary process detailed will show that the rosary is still in process. It is perfectly possible that the Angel's prayer of Fatima, *"O my Jesus, forgive us our sins; save us from the fires of Hell. Lead all souls to heaven, especially those who have most need of thy mercy,"* although presently used frequently in the rosary recitation, may become a permanent addition to each decade.

It must be said at this point that there can be no clear-cut analysis of the chronological succession in the development of the rosary. It is true that beads were first used to count psalms, then Our Fathers only, then Hail Marys only. Later the beads were used to count Our Fathers and Hail Marys together in various arrangements. Meditations on the mysteries of the rosary developed in various forms totally separate from the prayers. How all of this came together to form the contemporary rosary format is the story this book will unfold. This development did not happen through militia-like force but was, rather, a natural growth of popular devotion in which the various elements often existed side by side in various stages of development. As would be expected in a movement of popular devotion, considerable overlap of the various phases existed. Thus, this account of the various elements of the rosary story shows a development which twists and intermingles through time and place to produce a most satisfying and complete form of Christian devotion.

Introduction — Notes

1. J. G. Shaw, *The Story of the Rosary* (Milwaukee: The Bruce Publishing Company, 1954), p. 3.
2. Herbert Thurston, S.J., "Our Popular Devotions II: The Rosary," *The Month* 96 (1900), p. 405.
3. *Ibid.* An inscription is said to have still existed in the Church of *St. Maria in Campitelli* down to the last century. It ran as follows: "In nomine Domini, Amen. Anno 1217, Pontificatus Domini Honorii Papae, anno ejus secundo, indictione 6, mensis aprilis die 5, consecrata est ecclesia haec ab eodem summo pontifice et universall papa, per cujus sanctas manus, reconditae sunt in hoc altari Beatae Mariae Virginis multae reliquiae sanctorum et sanctarum, videlicet, de ligno Sanctae Crucis, de lacte, capillis et vestimentis gloriosae Virginis Mariae; item pars coronae de Pater noster Virginis Mariae." If this inscription is authentic and contemporary, it is an early instance both of the term *corona* and of the *Paternoster* to describe a string of beads.
4. Shaw, *Rosary*, p. 4.
5. Sir Monier Monier-Williams, *Hinduism* (London: Society for Promoting Christian Knowledge, 1878), pp. 61-62.
6. Ignaz Goldhizer, "Le Rosaire dans L'Islam," *Revue de l'- Histoire des Religions* 21 (1890), pp. 295-300.

7. *Ibid.*, p. 295.
8. *Ibid.*, p. 296.
9. Blessed Alanus de Rupe, O.P., was the person who made the association of St. Dominic with the rosary a standard in the tradition. In 1460, ten years before forming the rosary confraternity, Alanus wrote his account of Dominic's vision in a document currently kept in the archives of the Dominican order in Cologne, West Germany.
10. See *Acta Sanctorum* 32 (1733), p. 442ff.
11. See *Postquam Deo monente*, apostolic letter of Pope Pius IX, April 12, 1867; *Supremi apostolatus*, encyclical letter of Pope Leo XIII, September 1, 1883; *Novimus exiturum*, letter of Pope Pius X, June 27, 1908; *Fausto appetente die*, encyclical letter of Pope Benedict XV, June 29, 1921; *Inclytam ac perillustrem*, letter of Pope Pius XI, March 6, 1934. All of these documents make reference to St. Dominic as the originator of the rosary.
12. Thurston, "Popular Devotion: The Rosary," p. 404.
13. R. P. Devas, O.P., "The Rosary Tradition Defined and Defended," *American Catholic Quarterly Review* 41 (1916), pp. 128-47.
14. Interview with Father Hilary Martin, O.P., Dominican School of Philosophy and Theology, Berkeley, California, October 16, 1985.

Chapter 1
Historical Roots of the Rosary

When we speak of the rosary it seems unlikely that we should speak of hermits using stones, pegs or similar devices to count prayers. Yet this is where we must start our story since such practices are the forerunners of today's rosary beads. These hermits, the precursors of monasticism, were the first Christians to flee the world in their search for God. In their highly ascetical lifestyles, these hermits would spend many hours of each day in prayer. In order to count the prayers a particular hermit may have been designated to perform each day, some system was necessary. Thus, we find Sozomen, the early Church historian, writing in the fifth century about the hermit Paul of Egypt who lived in the mid-fourth century. Paul would fill his pocket with 300 pebbles and throw one away each time he said one of the 300 prayers he had set for himself that day.[1]

It was after these hermits, called anchorites, began to band together in community, spearheaded by the work of St. Pachomius (circa 290, one of the greatest of the monastic fathers), that distinct traces of the popular devotion which came to be known as the rosary came to the forefront. The common rule which characterized the monastic life was the great catalyst for a common method of counting prayers. Two twentieth-century historians, the aforementioned English Jesuit Herbert Thurston[2] and the German Canon F. M. Willam[3] both credit the Irish with initiating this particular phase of prayer counting which led to today's rosary.

The Psalter of the Lord

Our story begins with the psalms and their common recitation by the Irish monks. Since apostolic times the psalms of the Hebrew Scriptures have been used by Christians as a means of personal and communal prayer. When the Psalter became fixed it became common practice to divide the psalms into three groups of fifty psalms each. This grouping, known as the *Na tri coicat* (three fifties) was popular for both prayer and penance. Records show that by the year 800 the abbeys at Kemble and Canterbury required members to pray two "fifties" for the repose of the soul of each departed benefactor or monk.[4] In addition to their use in prayer for the dead, the *Na tri coicat* format was used as corporal prayer. A look at the life of St. Patrick gives good insight into this idea. A story is related that Patrick divided the night into three parts, the first two devoted to prayer and the third to sleep. He spent the time allotted to prayer reciting 100 psalms, two "fifties," and made 200 genuflections, one at the beginning and one at the end of each psalm. The second "fifty" he prayed while standing in cold water with arms extended in order to keep himself awake while performing penance.[5]

St. Columba is credited with bringing the use of the "fifties" to the European continent. Documentation shows that Irish influence on the "fifties" had spread to northern Italy by the mid-ninth century.[6] The very ascetic and corporal structure of using the "fifties" in prayer migrated along with the practice itself. Two monasteries, St. Gall and Reichenau, entered into an agreement for community prayer. On the death of any member from either monastery, the priests in both were obliged to offer a Mass and the other members to recite "fifty" for the soul of the departed member.[7] The monastery at Fulda, during the time of Charlemagne, petitioned the king to be allowed to retain the traditional obser-vance of the month's mind of St. Sturmius, the founder, by means of a vigil and the recitation of fifty psalms. The anniversary of the founding of the monastery was celebrated by a vigil and recitation of the entire Psalter, the three "fifties."[8]

The 150 psalms of the Hebrew Scriptures have comprised, since the earliest of Christian times, the most important part of the canonical hours. Recitation of the psalms and especially their reading was a practice in which only the intellectually elite could participate. Since the majority of people were illiterate and those that could read had difficulty getting access to a full text of the Latin psalms, something had to be done to allow the people to participate in the prayer of the Church. Memorization of the Psalter was considered too difficult and impracticable. Thus, the idea of a series of popular prayers was devised to allow participation by all people. Gradually over time the Psalter came to mean, over and above the psalms, a series of prayers composed of 150 individual parts. Later rosary development utilized this idea to its fullest as 150 *Paters* or *Aves* would be substituted for the psalms. During the early to late Middle Ages the Psalter was rearranged within the Divine Office so that all 150 psalms would be recited weekly.[9] For those people unable to use the Psalter for prayer, the substitution of popular prayers of the people allowed greater participation for all. This idea was manifest in the producing of books of 150 prayers so arranged in the vernacular to correspond with the weekly Psalter recitation.

The most natural progression of the popular prayers used in the recitation of the "fifties" was the introduction of the Jesus Psalter and consequently the formal use of the Our Father in prayer. The Jesus Psalter was a series of 150 prayers which sought to unveil the image of Christ in each of the 150 original psalms.[10] This series of meditations developed into an account of the life of Christ, telling in short phrases the principal events which took place from the Incarnation to the Ascension. The Irish were again the leaders in this development.

Because of the various ways in which a series of prayers

remembering the life of Jesus could be developed, a myriad of possibilities began to unfold. In order to bring some unity to the endless possibilities presented through meditation, the Irish monks, circa 750, started substituting *Paternosters* (Our Fathers) for the meditations or psalms assigned in penance.[11] Through this harmless shift to a well-known, biblically derived prayer, the development of the rosary took a major step toward being a prayer for the people. The importance of this shift cannot be overemphasized.

The practice of reciting Our Fathers in place of the psalms in prescribed numbers of fifty came to the European continent through the work of Irish monks. Thus we find the monastery at Cluny in 1096 decreeing that priest members should celebrate one Mass for each deceased member and those who were not priests should recite fifty psalms or fifty Our Fathers.[12] Similar practice is found in the Cistercian order of the twelfth century. Each member of the community was annually requested to recite the Psalter ten times, or the prayer *Miserere* or the Our Father 1,500 times. For each death in the community each monk was to recite the *Miserere* or the Our Father 150 times to correspond with the 150 psalm Psalter.[13]

The custom spread naturally to the medieval people as so many of them were bound economically and spiritually to close, day-to-day contact with the monks. Written records of such devotion among the laity are scant but it is known that this period produced the introduction of beads to count the prayers.[14] The practice became widespread and well-established. There is no doubt of the authenticity of William of Malmesbury's 1040 reference to Lady Godiva of Coventry, who bequeathed to the monastery founded by her a "circlet of gems which she had threaded on a string in order that by fingering them one-by-one as she successively recited her prayers, she might not fall short of the exact number."[15]

Additional evidence for the existence of prayer beads at the time is found in an inheritance case of 1151 in Würtemberg.[16] The discussion centered around whether or not the beads, referred to as "the counter," were to be considered a part of the personal property of the deceased or whether they belonged to the residue which returned to the community. The decision was made in favor of considering the beads as personal property. A short time later, an article appeared in the code of Saxon Law giving a widow the right to hold her "*Paternoster cord*" as a personal possession.[17]

Further evidence which shows this period to be formulative is the use of beads for counting Our Fathers, derived from analysis of the English language. The word *patter*, derived from *Paternoster*, has reference to those whose lips move rapidly and constantly as happens when someone recites the beads. In fact, the habit of calling the rosary a Paternoster became so firmly entrenched that the name remained popular long after the Hail Mary had become the principal prayer counted on beads. As late as 1496 a report from the Venetian embassy in London recorded that the English "all say Mass everyday, and say many *Paternosters* in public, the women carrying long strings of beads in their hands."[18]

Thus far we have traced the development of the rosary from a series of psalms to a repetitious recitation of the *Paternoster* counted on beads of some type. By the year 1000 the three "fifties" of Our Fathers known as the Little Psalter was in widespread use.[19] Both religious who were unable to use Latin and the laity found a great friend in the Little Psalter. Through this prayer devotion all Christian people were able to pray in communion with the Church according to their personal capability. The next major step in the process was the introduction of the Marian Psalter. The evolutionary development of this prayer has led to its major role in the present-day rosary.

The Psalter of Mary

Exactly where in history we have the right to apply the name *rosary* to the repetition of fifty or 150 prayers counted on beads is questionable; it depends on what one means by the term. If we hold to a strict contemporary definition of the rosary we must wait until the mid-sixteenth century, when the Hail Mary as we know it today took shape. However, if one sees the rosary as a series of meditations and repetitive prayers, then by our previous discussion we may have already reached that plateau in our development. Certainly, however, if one calls the devotion under discussion the rosary when it becomes a form of devotion to Mary, then the twelfth century might be a good date to choose. From this time abbreviated imitations of the Psalter, many with Marian themes, became very popular.[20]

It was natural in medieval times that shortened versions of the Psalter should find their form in devotion to Mary. The meditations on Jesus' life present in the Psalter could not be set forth without at the same time including the life of Mary; the two meditations were closely linked. The great devotion to Mary found in the twelfth century resulted in a succession of Marian Psalters presenting 150 praises of the Virgin often in the *Na tri coicat* format. As the custom of reciting 150 brief verses in honor of Mary became more and more common, the close connection with the psalms was laid aside. This devotion became in essence a saluting of Mary 150 times with no standard act of corporal prayer. Ultimately, with the formation of the original Hail Mary, the Marian Psalter became a series of *Aves* recited rapidly with little devotional strength.

The replacement of the Our Father with the Hail Mary occurred through complex processes in the eleventh and twelfth centuries.[21] This development was headed by the efforts of several archbishops of Canterbury who composed "Psalters of 150 Praises of the Blessed Virgin,"[22] many of which used the *Ave* as the basic repetitive prayer. In the thirteenth century various English dioceses (following the example of the French) required the faithful to memorize the *Ave Maria*.[23] As time progressed the Little Psalter and beads became increasingly associated with the Virgin Mary.

Recitation of *Aves* in a format similar to today's rosary spread rapidly throughout the Church world. The story is told of the hermit Aybert in Hennegau (died 1140) who recited the Hail Mary 150 times each day. The first one hundred *Aves* he made genuflections, and the last fifty he prostrated himself on the ground.[24] As early as the eleventh century St. Anselm is credited with the collection of 150 quatrains, each beginning with the salutation *Ave Maria*.[25] The work is divided into three parts of fifty quatrains, each imitating the *Na tri coicat* format of the Psalter.

Numerous stories, some apocryphal, some true, abound in the literature describing the spread of devotion to Mary through the use of the Hail Mary. One legend recorded widely during this period tells the amusing story of Eulalia, who was very devoted to the Blessed Virgin. One day our Lady appeared to the holy woman. Although Eulalia was at first alarmed, the legend tells us that the apparition reassured her in the following words:

> Do not, my daughter, be afraid of the fond Mother to whom each weekday you pay all homage in your power. But I caution you that if you wish the services you render me to benefit yourself more and to be more acceptable to me, then do not in the future pronounce the words [of the Hail Mary] so rapidly, for let me tell you that when you greet me with the Angelical Salutation, I experience a great thrill of joy, and more especially when you utter lingeringly the words *Dominus tecum* [the Lord is with you]. The delight I feel then is more than can be expressed in words. For then it seems to me that I feel my Son within me even as He, true God and man, was with me when he vouchsafed to be born of me for the sake of sinners. And as this was an unspeakable joy for me at that time, so is it now when *Dominus tecum* is said to me in the Angelical Salutation.
>
> On hearing this, that handmaid of Christ was filled with intense delight, and to her sweetest Mother she offered countless thanksgivings with manifold prayers in return for the loving consolation and the kindly admonition which had been given her. And thus the Mother of all nature, departing from her, returned amid great glory to the heavenly kingdom, where, as we believe, she remains with her Son forever. Finally, that sister, wishing to make the prayers which she was wont to say more pleasing to Our Lady St. Mary and more profitable to herself, she straightway set to work to shorten them. For the practice which she was wont to follow was this, that every day for the love of her she repeated without interruption *Ave Maria gratia plena Dominus tecum* as many times as she had heard that there were psalms in the psalter, and in order to complete the entire number each day she had to pronounce the Angelic *Ave* more rapidly than she should. But now, encouraged by this admonition from the Mother of Our Lord, she gave up reciting two-thirds of what she had formerly said and made a

practice of pronouncing the remaining third with great earnestness and more deliberately.[26]

This story is significant regardless of its historical reality. The important idea is that at the time the story was written down, the devotion referred to in it was already known and practiced.

There are numerous records of people who recited a specific number of *Aves* each day, usually in the now somewhat traditional unit of fifty. These prayers were many times accompanied by a gesture of respect or penance. The same twelfth century British museum manuscript which speaks of Eulalia also tells of a man who, every time he passed our Lady's altar, "had the habit of saluting her with reverence and saying Hail Mary full of grace, the Lord is with thee."[27] Another more factual account speaks of St. Louis, King of France, who knelt down fifty times each evening in prayer. Each time he stood upright again and then knelt down he would slowly pray an *Ave Maria*.[28]

It is interesting to analyze the Dominican rosary tradition and practice during the same thirteenth century period. Dominican Brother Romeo, a contemporary of St. Dominic, would recite daily while kneeling 1,000 Hail Marys counted on a knotted cord.[29] Blessed Margaret of Hungary, O.P., had the custom of reciting prostrate on the ground 1,000 Our Fathers on nights of feasts of Our Lord and 1,000 Hail Marys on the eve of feasts of our Lady.[30] These examples show that the Dominicans were early promoters of the Hail Mary. The absence, however, of any reference to 150 *Aves* is very surprising if one accepts the hypothesis that St. Dominic was the first promoter of the rosary, receiving it from the Virgin Mary herself.

The Marian Psalter and the Rose Garden

As has been described, the evolutionary process which brought the Hail Mary to replace the Our Father in the repetitious prayers of "fifties" was a very complex one. One of the most intriguing and interesting associations in the development of today's rosary is the connection between the Hail Mary, a *rosarium* (rose garden) and the prayer beads. What exactly is the affiliation of these seemingly diverse ideas and from where do they originate?

From a scriptural point of view our search must begin in the Song of Songs with its garden scene. In this garden of Solomon, a garden of peace, a woman lives as the "rose of Sharon, the lily of the valleys" (Songs 2:1). The poem, considered by Christians as an epithalamium for the nuptials between Christ and his beloved, is truly a prefiguring of the Virgin Mary. "You are all fair my love; there is no flaw in you" (Songs 4:7). In a similar way the garden of this poem prefigures the rose garden of Mary. "A garden locked is my sister, my bride; a garden locked, a fountain sealed" (Songs 4:12). The garden in Song of Songs was considered by medievals as a *locus secretus*, a place of immortality where roses never die.[31] Such gardens were regularly depicted in art full of ornamental birds, usually peacocks.

As mentioned previously, devotion to the Blessed Virgin Mary was firmly entrenched in the medieval Church. The rose garden, with its peacocks symbolizing immortality, its water of life and its singing birds soon became a symbol of that which was beyond the realm of death. In parts of Germany graveyards were called rose gardens because the roses planted there were an allusion to paradise.[32]

During the twelfth century the rose symbolism and its association with Mary began to take a major place in the tradition. Aided by the preaching of St. Bernard of Clairvaux and others in the Cistercian order, the rose garden became a symbol of the beauty, wisdom and mysteriousness of the Virgin Mary. An apocryphal story of the period shows the contemporary mind-set. A knight upon entering a monastery as a lay brother would daily sew a garland of roses for our Lady. He found, however, after some time that his duties in the monastery left no time for weaving the garland. He consulted a wise older monk who told him, "Our Lady would be even more pleased if you would say *Aves* each day for her crown of roses."[33] Various versions of this story from Spanish and Carthusian influence became important links between roses and Marian devotion. From this connection arose many Marian

Psalters with garden motifs. Examples of these prayer devotions include the *Hortus Deliciarum* (The Garden of Delights) by Herrad of Landsberg, the *Rosarium Philosophorium* by Arnold of Villanova (circa 1290) and *Rosarium Jesu*, a Benedictine book of fifty rhymed prayers.[34]

The application of the term *rosarium*, rose garden, to the prayer beads had its major development in the fourteenth and fifteenth centuries. During this period the rose, rose garden, rose bush and rose garland all became symbols alluding to the Marian Psalter, and then, gradually with even more explicit reference, to the prayer beads. By the middle of the fifteenth century the concept of a rose garden and a wreath of roses was firmly established as symbolizing the Mystic Rose of Scripture — the Virgin Mary. The rosary beads became formally incorporated into this whole structure with the decree of Pope Gregory XIII in 1573 establishing the Feast of the Rosary.[35]

Prayer Counters

To this point in our discussion we have been concerned with the development of various Psalters as forerunners of the basic prayers and format to today's rosary. Without question, the rosary is most fundamentally a series of repetitive prayers and meditations. Yet the only physical evidence we see when one prays the rosary are the beads themselves. As alluded to throughout the text, numerous types of counters have been used to count prayers. The sheer number of *Aves*, *Paters* and meditations necessitates some means of counting.

The first efforts in Christendom to count prayers date back to the Desert Fathers. The ascetics who fled to the desert to achieve some type of spiritual martyrdom were the followers of St. Paul's exhortation to pray always. These men and women would memorize the psalms and at least one Gospel (usually the Gospel of Mark was chosen because of its relative brevity). Each hermit would determine the number of psalms and/or prayers to be recited each day. Paul of Thebes (circa 234-347) is thought to be the first to use a pile of pebbles, shifting the stones one by one to a second pile as his daily quota of prayers was completed.[36] This same idea continued in practice for centuries as we find St. Clare in the eleventh century using a similar technique for her prayer life due to a lack of string or beads.[37] Other primitive methods of counting prayers during this period were tying knots in string or making notches in a stick. The element of moving stones or notching sticks added a rhythmical physical movement to the strenuous mental exercise and discipline of prayer.

By the mid to late medieval period more sophisticated methods for prayer counting came into common use. These new methods had one common quality: they were all devices which could be used over and over again. Unlike transferring or discarding pebbles or notching a stick, the new methods, prompted by more widespread participation in such repetitive prayer devotions, provided devices which, once made, could be used to count prayers by fingering various knots or beads. The circlet of gems which Lady Godiva bequeathed to a Benedictine priory in 1041 were threaded on a string in order that by fingering them one by one she could recite the precise number of prayers. Her instructions to the monastery when presenting the gift were that the gems were to be hung as a necklace on a statue of the Virgin Mary — *collo imaginis Sancta Mariae appendi.*[38] By the middle of the twelfth century it was common for people to have a string of beads or a knotted cord on their person at all times in order to count *Paternosters* or *Aves*. As mentioned earlier, the code of Saxon Law gave people the right to carry their "*Paternoster* cord" as a personal possession. This is verified by adjudication of a will at Isny in Algau (Würtemberg) where records show a "*Paternoster* cord" was awarded to the family of the deceased.[39]

Prayer counters are not solely a Roman Catholic tradition. The Greek Orthodox *kombologion* is a woolen cord of 103 knots which is divided into four equal parts of twenty-five by three large beads, leaving a pendant of three knots which terminates in a little cross-shaped tassel.[40] The kombologion became in many ways the prototype counter for the modern rosary once the number and type of prayers were fixed.

Summary

The historical derivation of the rosary begins with the Desert Fathers and their primitive yet laborious systems of repetitive prayer. Through the ascetic lifestyles of these men and women a style of prayer was born. The first major step in our story begins with the Irish monks in the seventh century. At this time the 150 psalms of the Hebrew Scriptures were divided into a *Na tri coicat* format of three groups of fifty psalms. Arranged in such a way, the "fifties" served both as reflective and corporal/penitential prayer.

The need for lay participation in the prayer of the Church produced the need for a Psalter of the Lord, a Psalter that could be prayed by all, not merely the intellectually elite. Thus the practice of substituting *Paternosters* for psalms became popular with the Irish, who brought the custom to mainland Europe. Ultimately, because of the inevitable interface and interaction between the worship of Jesus and devotion to Mary, popular devotion forced *Aves* to replace *Paternosters* in the same *Na tri coicat* format. Spurred by the association of Mary with roses and rose gardens, both from a scriptural base and by many legends, the Marian Psalter became by the fourteenth century the standard form of repetitive prayer in the life of laity, clergy and religious alike.

With the evolution of repetitive prayer forms came the need for a method to count the many prayers. Starting with simple pebbles and wood notches the counters became more sophisticated, so that by the twelfth century it was common for all people to carry a "*Paternoster* cord" on their person for purposes of keeping straight the prayers recited on any group of fifty.

At the dawn of the fifteenth century the rosary as we know it today could not be recognized. A series of *Aves* (not the complete Hail Mary of today) recited over and over again together with a cord of knots or stringed gems or beads was the format at that time. The fifteenth and sixteenth centuries would, however, advance the rosary from popular devotion to official recognition by the Church.

Chapter 1 — Notes

1. Sozomen, *The Ecclesiastical History*, trans. Edward Walford (London: G. Bohn, 1855), p. 32.
2. Herbert Thurston, S.J., "Rosary," *Catholic Encyclopedia* vol. 13 (New York: Robert Appleton Company, 1907), p. 185.
3. Franz Michel Willam, *The Rosary: Its History and Meaning*, trans. Edwin Kaiser, C.PP.S. (New York: Benziger Brothers, 1953), pp. 12-13.
4. Thurston, "Rosary," p. 185.
5. Martin P. Harney, S.J., *The Legacy of Saint Patrick* (Boston: The Daughters of St. Paul, 1972), p. 103.
6. Irish monasticism spread to the European continent beginning in the fifth century with St. Patrick. Italy came under Irish monastic influence soon thereafter. See Anselmo M. Tommasini, *Irish Saints in Italy*, trans. J. F. Scanlan (London: Sands and Company, 1937), especially pp. 63-127.
7. J. G. Shaw, *The Story of the Rosary* (Milwaukee: The Bruce Publishing Company, 1954), p. 18.
8. Dominikus Heller, *Quellenstudien zur Friihgeshichte des Klosters Fulda* (Fulda: Verlag, Parzeller & Co.), pp. 32-33.
9. The full Psalter of 150 psalms recited weekly was common practice, especially among monastic orders, by the mid-twelfth century.
10. This Psalter took verses or strophes of each psalm and ar-

ranged them with some characteristic theme or idea of Jesus. Although not as difficult as memorizing the psalms, these prayers never were in common use because of the amount of memorization required.

11. See Oscar D. Watkins, *A History of Penance*, vol. 2 (New York: Burt Franklin, 1961), p. 757. The penitentials used by Irish priests became the standard of use from the eighth century as Irish monasticism paved the way for private confession.

12. Noreen Hunt, *Cluny Under Saint Hugh 1049-1109* (London: Edward Arnold LTD, Publishers, 1967), pp. 99-107.

13. Louis J. Lekai, *The Cistercian's Ideals and Reality* (Kent, OH: Kent State University Press, 1977), pp. 248-53.

14. As alluded to in the introduction, it is probable that parallel developments in prayer counters were present for Christians and Moslems. Both faiths needed counters to assure proper recitation of the many daily prayers said by an individual.

15. Herbert Thurston, S.J., "Our Popular Devotions: The Rosary," *The Month* 96 (1900), p. 406.

16. Shaw, *Rosary*, pp. 18-9.

17. Otto Mayer, *Das Staatsrecht des Konigreichs Sachsen* (Tubingen: J. C. B. Mohr, 1909), p. 104.

18. Shaw, *Rosary*, p. 19.

19. The Little Psalter and the Little Office of the Blessed Virgin Mary were popular prayer methods at this time. This was a method to pray with the whole Church and not have to read or have memorized the psalms.

20. The historical roots of the Marian Psalter can be derived from a desire to have a prayer form utilized by the whole Church. Since the Hail Mary was beginning to take form as a prayer, the natural progression was to use it as a substitute for the psalms in the *Na tri coicat* format.

21. As popular devotion to Mary became normative in Church practice, the Hail Mary became the natural successor to the Our Father as the basic prayer for the Psalter.

22. Shaw, *Rosary*, p. 28.

23. *Ibid.*, p. 38.

24. Willam, *The Rosary*, p. 24.
25. Eadmer, *The Life of St. Anselm*, trans. R. W. Southern (London: Thomas Nelson and Sons, LTD, 1962), pp. 121-22.
26. Thurston, "Our Popular Devotions II: The Rosary," p. 411.
27. *Ibid.*, p. 412.
28. Herbert Thurston, S.J., "Hail Mary," *Catholic Encyclopedia*, vol. 7 (New York: Robert Appleton, 1910), p. 111.
29. Herbert Thurston, S.J., "Our Popular Devotions II: The Rosary V," *The Month* 97 (1901), p. 173.
30. *Ibid.*
31. See R. Gribble, "Roses of October," *Queen of All Hearts* (November-December 1986), pp. 18-19. The garden of immortality is described in literature and art of the period as the place where the Virgin Mary would live as the unblemished bride of Songs 4:12.
32. In parts of Germany today one can see "Rosengartens" which are graveyards. The concept of immortality, represented by roses, carried over to a place where the dead were buried in hopes of eternal life.
33. Thurston, "Our Popular Devotions: The Rosary II; The Rosary Amongst the Carthusians," *The Month* 96 (1900), p. 520.
34. Eithne Wilkins, *The Rose-Garden Game* (London: Victor Gollancz, LTD, 1969), p. 106.
35. Adolf Adam, *The Liturgical Year*, trans. Matthew J. O'-Connell (New York: Pueblo Publishing Company, 1981), p. 221.
36. See note 1.
37. Sister Mary Seraphim, P.C.P.A., *Clare: Her Light and Her Song* (Chicago: Franciscan Herald Press, 1984), p. 48. Also see *Francis and Clare*, The Classics of Western Spirituality Series (Paulist Press, 1982).
38. Wilkins, *Rose-Garden*, p. 25.
39. Willam, *The Rosary*, p. 18.
40. Wilkins, *Rose-Garden*, p. 5.

Chapter 2
The Rosary Develops

The fifteenth century dawned with much hope and fresh thought for a world that had long been mired in a period of cultural, social and political drought. The age of the Renaissance was coming to Europe and with it the thoughts of all people turned to the new and possible. Great advances in art, music and similar expressive trades brought people to a new and fresh awareness of the possibilities that were waiting to be achieved. Religious thought and practice were not excluded from this great awakening. It was during the fifteenth and ensuing centuries that the rosary took shape and became a recognized devotion within the Roman Catholic tradition.

The Dominican Tradition and Apocrypha

Although the fifteenth century saw the major developments which would result in recognition of the rosary as a standard form of devotion, our story must continue with the tradition that existed at that time. The aforementioned legend of St. Dominic and his association with the rosary was the reigning story captivating most all the faithful with its beauty and simplicity. Strange as it seems, the legend of St. Dominic did not originate during the saint's lifetime nor even during the century in which he lived. Some stories certainly existed during the thirteenth century which connected Dominic to the prayer, but it was not until the mid-fifteenth century that Alanus de Rupe, a name we will see again, made the legend common knowledge. Rupe, a Dominican monk, wrote an account of a vision in which our Lady appeared to St. Dominic, revealing to him the devotion to the prayer and entrusting him with the task of promulgating it.[1]

Combining fact and legend, Rupe's story would sound much like the following saga. Dominic, working aggressively and diligently in his fight for preservation of the Church, was dejected for his apparent failure to convert the Cathars to orthodox Christianity. In 1214, the saint returned to a cave in the wilderness near Toulouse. There, exhausted after three days of penitential fasting and prayer, he collapsed and had a vision. The Virgin Mary appeared to him accompanied by three queens and fifty maidens — the numbers clearly corresponding to the pattern of the Psalter. Mary raised him up from his prostrate position, kissed him, and in the style of medieval erotic mysticism, quenched his thirst with milk from her chaste breasts. She told Dominic that intellectual thinking and preaching were not required against the Cathars, but rather, the successful promotion and use of her Psalter. At that time, says the legend, Mary gave Dominic a rosary, instructing him on its use against the Cathars.[2] Although this story, as suggested earlier, cannot be historically proven or supported, it very quickly became part and parcel of the rosary tradition as it simply and effectively gave acceptability to the devotion by its direct association with a highly regarded saint from a believable past.

Modern scholarship on St. Dominic's life has given a new twist to the classic tale generated by Alanus de Rupe. Manuscripts found in some European Dominican priories state that Dominic's use of the rosary came as a result of inspiration from Mary in combating the heresies of the Albigensians in Southern France.[3] Dominic, state the manuscripts, would use three of the greatest mysteries of the Gospel, Incarnation, Redemption, and Eternal Life, in his preaching against the heretics. Father Reginald Garrigou-Lagrange, the renowned Dominican theologian, stated in an article in *Doctrine and Life* for October-November, 1952 that:

> Under the inspiration of Mary, St. Dominic saw that in order to bring back the souls led astray by the Albigenses, who were falsifying all the mysteries of salvation, it was necessary to put before them these mysteries in their truth, not however in the abstract way of catechism but in a concrete and living form as the Gospel itself does. Only by this means can faith be rendered truly firm and vital, penetrating and practical, able to savor the mysteries it accepts and communicate them to others. Now what are these mysteries of salvation revealed to us in the Gospel? They are the three great mysteries of the Incarnation, the Redemption and Eternal Life. St. Dominic then under the inspiration of Our Lady, preached in the heretical villages the mysteries according to the Gospel itself.[4]

The story of St. Dominic's involvement with the rosary may have begun in the fifteenth century but it has been advanced, fostered and promulgated from the time of Alanus de Rupe forward. There was every reason why the belief should be accepted. It had been set down in the breviary and the Second Nocturn of Matins on the Feast of the Most Holy Rosary.[5] Even the most scholarly people, like Cardinal John Henry Newman, accepted the story unquestioningly.[6] Acceptance of the story was repeated in official papal statements over a period of 400 years. Pope Leo XIII, the most vocal papal advocate of the rosary, explicitly stated in at least seven of his pronouncements between 1883 and 1901 that St. Dominic instituted the rosary. In one encyclical, *Magnae Dei Matris* (September 8, 1892), the pope stated,

> The well-known origins of the rosary, illustrated in monuments of which we have made frequent mention, bears witness to its remarkable efficacy. For, in the days when the Albigensian sect, posing as champion of pure faith and morals, but in reality introducing the worst kind of anarchy and corruption, brought many a nation to its utter ruin, the Church fought against it and the other infamous factions associated with it, not with troops and arms, but chiefly with the power of the most holy rosary, the rite of which the Mother of God taught to our Father Dominic in order that he might propagate it.[8]

The story of St. Dominic and the rosary went virtually unchallenged until the eighteenth century and the work of the Bollandists. This group of Jesuit theologians sought to discover the truth concerning the lives of the saints. In their work they could find no substantive historical data to verify the legend which had been prominent for hundreds of years. There was no question that there was a close association between the Dominicans and the rosary, especially its promotion, but the historical evidence was lacking to show its origins with St. Dominic himself.

Reaction to the Bollandists' position was swift to defend the tradition. Although written much later, an article by R. P. Devas, O.P., in the *American Catholic Quarterly Review* is typical of the defensive position:

> Not only is the name of St. Dominic in question, not only is the wisdom of the seventeen Sovereign Pontiffs at stake — nay even the very common sense of at least five of them [those who wrote after the Bollandists] — but the fair name and fame of Our Blessed Lady herself are also, as must be admitted, most deeply involved. For if the rosary does indeed come to us from her, if it really is a gift from her virginal hands, surely the very least we can do is gratefully to acknowledge it. Nay, on the supposition that Our Lady did deign to reveal this devotion to St. Dominic, it would be all but an insult on our part deliberately to ignore it. For this reason, therefore, in the first place, and also on account of the unfounded statements on the subject which occasionally appear in the Catholic press, I propose to examine in the following pages the truth of this old tradition.[9]

Father Devas strongly advances the traditional story but cannot prove what he states. From a purely historical discussion his statement cannot be verified.

Other Dominican authors began to show more respect for the historical argument. Father Bede Jarrett, O.P., in his *Life of St. Dominic* spent little time with the legend. He certainly holds that St. Dominic preached the rosary of Our Fathers and Hail Marys (this form was not present, however, in the thirteenth century) but limits his claims as originator to the aspect of devotion. Credit for the actual origin of the rosary is ascribed to tradition. He writes,

It [the rosary] comprised the saying of Our Fathers and Hail Marys which were checked and noted by a string of beads, a contrivance, of course, older even than Christianity, and already widespread over Europe before his time. St. Dominic did not invent these things, though it would seem that he popularized them. To him, however, a papal tradition points as the originator of the division into decades or groups of ten, separated by larger beads called *Paternosters*. Under the influence of the Order these chaplets, at this date, spread widely over Christendom, and are to be found carved [sic] on tombs, and are from St. Dominic's time alluded to in devotional literature.[10]

Without question the most significant and uncontested fact about St. Dominic and his Order of Preachers concerning the rosary is its promotion of the prayer since the inception of the order. In *Liber Sacramentorum*, Cardinal Ildefonso Schuster states, "it is to the Dominican Order that the glory must be given of having propagated this prayer with such success that the rosary rapidly became the most popular devotion in Christendom."[11] Dominican history is full of stories which promoted the rosary to a place of prominence in popular devotion. This is the only really significant idea that matters. Historical evidence may not support Dominic's role as originator of the rosary but the legend is useful, nevertheless, in its effect of bringing more prominence and attention to this special prayer devotion.

St. Dominic and his vision of Mary is not the only legend concerning the origin of the rosary, although it is certainly the most widespread and popular. A Scottish manuscript from Auchinleck, circa 1310, tells of the origin of the Psalter of 150 *Aves*. There was a certain youth who had the habit of reciting fifty Hail Marys in honor of our Lady. Then one day Mary appeared to him and told him to pray the fifty Hail Marys three times every day, morning, noon and evening. He was to count the prayers on his fingers, ten by ten, and after each ten sing a hymn to her. As she appeared to him poorly clad, Mary pointed out that this was because her prayers were so short. The youth promptly harkened to her advice and recited 150 *Aves* every day from that day forward. On the seventh day thereafter, the Blessed Virgin appeared to the youth again, clothed this time as a bride on her wedding day, and thanked him for his prayers.[12]

Another fable concerning the Marian Psalter circulated through France, Spain and Germany during the thirteenth century. The story states that the Virgin appeared before a praying monk and, taking the prayers from his lips and turning them into roses, made a wreath of roses. The tale usually speaks of the prayers being fifty *Aves*. In different versions of the story Mary would wear the wreath; other times, she would give it to the monk to wear.[13]

A third Marian legend related to the rosary speaks of Mary's request that the *Aves* be said in a reflective mood. The story has Mary say, "As often as men honor me with the Angelic Salutation I feel a joy well up in me at the words, 'the Lord is with thee,' a joy which cannot be described."[14]

The Prayers Develop

The rosary is a devotion of prayers and meditations which are counted on, and thereby unified by, a string of beads formed in a specific pattern. So far in our discussion the Our Father and Hail Mary have been mentioned numerous times without qualification. It is true that the Our Father as we know it today (slight textual modification exempted) is directly drawn from St. Matthew's Gospel when Jesus taught his disciples to pray (Matthew 6:9-13). The other prayers of today's rosary, although scripturally based, are not drawn directly from the Bible, but rather like the rosary itself, came to their present state through an evolutionary process. The fifteenth century was the period when great strides were made in establishing the prayers which are so common to Roman Catholics today.

As we have noted, by the dawn of the fifteenth century the Marian Psalter and its use of the Hail Mary was in popular practice. The Hail Marys used then and now, however, are different prayers. If the Our Father came to be by God coming to the people, then the Hail Mary, as we know it today, came into existence through the people going to God by borrowing the prayers of the Church to honor Jesus' mother.

In its pre-fifteenth century form the Hail Mary consisted entirely of the salutation of Gabriel plus what St. Peter Damian called the "evangelical" salutation of Elizabeth.[15] The angel Gabriel states in Luke 1:28, "Hail, O favored one, the Lord is with you. Blessed are you among women." Elizabeth, representing the human race's response to Mary's powerful sign, begins her words by saying, "Blessed are you among women and blessed is the fruit of your womb" (Luke l:42).

These two passages seem to naturally join together and have been so united since the patristic period. These two greetings are first seen joined in the Offertory of the Mass for the fourth Sunday of Advent, which had been a Marian celebration since the year 600.[16] The salutation of Mary is used in some form in several rituals of that period or earlier. The Saturday Divine Office in honor of Mary and the Little Office of Mary both contained the greetings of Gabriel and Elizabeth.[17] Also, the Elizabethan greeting was used as an antiphon at vespers and lauds. Although the greetings were evidently used during this period, there is no sign that these combined passages were used as a separate prayer on its own.

Despite the apparent lack of independence for this prayer, the pious literature of the medieval period has provided us with a legend, which like that of St. Dominic involves an apparition of our Lady and credits the origin of the Hail Mary as a separate prayer to one of Mary's great servants. In this instance the legend concerns St. Ildephonsus, Archbishop of Toledo, who died in 667. The legend states that one evening the archbishop entered his cathedral and found our Lady sitting on his own episcopal chair with a choir of angels around her singing praise. As Ildephonsus approached the scene, he fashioned his own praises to join in the angels' chorus. Making a series of genuflections, Ildephonsus repeated the words of the angel Gabriel's greeting — "Hail Mary, full of grace, the Lord is with thee. Blessed art thou among women and blessed is the fruit of thy womb." To show her pleasure at this homage, our Lady presented the archbishop with a beautiful chasuble.[18] This legend, recounted by Mabillon in his *Acta* of the Saints of the Benedictine order,[19] gives us the two salutations joined to form the Hail Mary as it existed to the fifteenth century.

It is not possible to determine exactly when the Hail Mary became an officially recognized prayer but evidence points to efforts beginning in the tenth century.[20] The aforementioned Little Office of the Blessed Virgin Mary became a very popular devotion. Although there is no specific evidence that this Little Office initiated the joining of the two phrases of Gabriel and Elizabeth, it is clear that their use together as a separate prayer followed shortly thereafter. Mention of a separate Marian prayer is contained in the works of St. Peter Damian, who died in 1072. Peter speaks of a cleric who had fallen away from his vocation but had preserved the habit of reciting each day before a statue of our Lady the words: "Hail Mary, full of grace, the Lord is with thee. Blessed art thou among women and blessed is the fruit of thy womb."[21] We know from other legends of the period that the angelic salutation became quite a common prayer though we cannot be certain to what extent the *Aves* consisted of both salutations. We do have dated evidence of the change from one salutation to a combination of both in at least one place. In 1184, a Cistercian abbot named Baldwin, later an archbishop of Canterbury, wrote, "To this salutation of the angel, by which we daily greet the most Blessed Virgin, with such devotion as we may, we are accustomed to add the words, 'and blessed is the fruit of thy womb,' by which clause Elizabeth at a later time, on hearing the Virgin's salutation to her, caught up and completed, as it were the Angel's words, saying, 'Blessed art thou among women and blessed is the fruit of thy womb.' "[22]

Up to this period there is no mention in any of the diocesan regulations of the Hail Mary as an official prayer. In the late twelfth century (1198), the prayer is listed along with the Creed and the Our Father in a synodal decree of the bishops of Paris.[23] This was followed by similar decrees at Durham (1217), Treves (1227), Coventry (1237), Valence (1255), and Norwich (1257).[24]

As the biblical roots for the Hail Mary became exhausted, the popular devotion of the laity began to expand the prayer to its present form. The first significant addition is the name of Jesus at the end of the original prayer. Although the practice was seemingly not followed for at least 200 years, it is believed that Pope Urban IV in 1261 was the first to add the word Jesus at the end of the Elizabethan salutation to Mary.[25] Records show that an indulgence was granted for such a practice.[26] Why this simple yet important addition to the prayer was not in common use by the fifteenth century can only be hypothesized. However, it is thought by Thurston, among other rosary scholars, that the record of the indulgence was lost for a period, surfacing only in the late fifteenth century.[27] A prayer book entitled *Der Seelen Trost* (Soul's Consolation), published in 1474, recognizes the addition of the name Jesus in the prayer text.[28] The prayer book divides the Hail Mary into four parts: (1) the greeting of the angel Gabriel, (2) the greeting of Elizabeth, (3) the holy name of Jesus Christ and (4) the Amen. At the close of the fifteenth century the prayer book *Imitation of Christ*, printed at Rome in 1498, became the standard for the Hail Mary form:

Hail Mary full of grace, the Lord is with thee. Blessed art thou among women and blessed is the fruit of thy womb, Jesus Christ. Amen.[29]

Although the then known Hail Mary was scripturally based and had been accepted by many then prominent theologians and church officials, the power of the people would not be denied in bringing the prayer to greater fullness. Much of the initiative for a more "complete" prayer came from the reformers and their followers in the sixteenth century. This was the time when the private devotion with which we are all familiar, "Holy Mary, Mother of God, pray for us sinners, now and at the hour of our death," was added. The origins of this prayer devotion, however, as with the whole story of the rosary, are diverse and complex.

Our first evidence for the private addition to the Hail Mary is found in the documents of the Council of Ephesus in 431.[30] Ephesus was famous for its definition of the Blessed Virgin Mary as the Theotokos, Mother of God, refuting the position of Nestorius and his followers. Although the debates of Ephesus were based on christological issues, it is understandable that the phrase, "Holy Mary, Mother of God, pray for us sinners," could come from documents defining the role of the Blessed Virgin Mary.

Using the words formed at Ephesus, the prayer of petition at the end of the Hail Mary began to develop from the thirteenth century.[31] During this century it became quite common to add invocations to Mary in prayer devotions. This was regularly practiced in such prayers as the *Alma Redemptoris Mater*, the *Ave Regina Coelorum* and the offices such as the Little Office of Mary.[32] The specific form seen in the Hail Mary can be traced from Italy. One example that was falsely attributed to Dante but certainly belongs to fourteenth century Italy goes as follows:

> O virgin blessed do thou always
> Pray for us to God that he may pardon
> And give us grace so to live that he
> Will grant paradise at our death.[33]

St. Anselm of Canterbury (a native Italian) wrote a petition very similar to the above prayer.[34] An English translation of the French Shepherd's Calendar of 1493 gives the following petition: "Holy Mary moder [sic] of God, praye [sic] for us synners [sic]. Amen."[35] Back in Italy, a short work written by the Catholic reformer Savonarola in 1495 is prefaced by a Hail Mary which is just one word away from our own. It ends, "Holy Mary, mother of God, pray for us sinners now and at the hour of death. Amen."[36] In the same year, the Camaldolese monks of Italy added a private petition in the breviaries almost exactly as written by Savonarola.[37] Additionally, we find in 1499 a petition in an instruction by the archbishop of Mainz, Berthold von Hennebert, in the following form: "Holy Mary, mother of God, pray for us now and at the hour of death. Amen."[38]

Although various forms of this prayer petition continued to be used in the first half of the sixteenth century, the official "Catechism of the Council of Trent" placed its approval on the petition wording we know today. The catechism gives the wording, "Holy Mary, mother of God, pray for us sinners now and at the hour of our death. Amen."[39] The council concluded, "Most rightly has the holy Church of God added to this thanksgiving petition the invocation of the most holy mother of God, thereby implying that we should piously and suppliantly have recourse to her in order that by her intercession she may reconcile God with us sinners and obtain for us the blessings we need both for this present life and for the life which has no end."[40]

The strictly official adoption of the Hail Mary in its present form came with its publication in the Roman Breviary of 1568.[41] Tradition and local custom allowed the older forms to linger on for years within several private communities. Dominican tradition, for example, preserved for a long period the custom of saying the Hail Mary in its short form as an antiphon on one of the three small beads of the pendant before beginning the rosary proper.[42] Herbert Thurston reported that as late as 1900 people in Ireland when told to say Hail Marys for a penance would ask, "Must we say the Holy Mary too?"[43] Despite some minor variations Catholics today are united in their recitations of the Hail Mary.

The importance of the Hail Mary has been recognized by the Church from the origins of the prayer. The scholastic age was, however, the period where recognition was made by important scholars and theologians of the time. St. Albert the Great and his protege St. Thomas Aquinas used the original shortened version of the prayer as the basis for several homilies. Albert wrote, "Mary and we should greet each other often. We should greet her because we want to have her greet us too."[44] Recognition of the importance of the prayer is seen in its constant use. Beginning with the diocese of Paris in 1198, there were thirteen dioceses that by 1354 had made the prayer mandatory knowledge for all the faithful.[45] In such a vein, a comment by the German preacher Berthold of Regensburg (died 1272) is appropriate: "If they [the faithful] are able to understand the Hail Mary as well, that is a great wonder."[46] Popular devotion and official church practice have brought the Hail Mary to its rightful position of prominence. Its use as the primary prayer of the rosary is, therefore, most appropriate and proper.

The doxology or "Glory be to the Father. . ." recited at the conclusion of each decade of the rosary has an origin much different than the Hail Mary although, as previously seen, an evolutionary development of the prayer is present. One thing is certain of the doxology, its origin and derivation in prayer is much older than any part of the rosary excepting the Our Father which is, of course, a prayer that Jesus taught to the disciples. Roots for a doxology, which praises God, can be found in the Hebrew Scriptures. "God be praised" was a popular doxology for the Israelite community. For Christians it was only natural that God, Father, Son and Spirit should be praised. Thus, the invocation of the Trinity was common practice in the early patristic period. St. Basil (died 379) stated that the doxology, "Glory be to the Father, to the Son and to the Holy Spirit," was derived from ancient tradition.[47] This would indicate that most probably the invocation of the Trinity originated in apostolic times.

Regular use of such a doxology was promoted through the common prayer of the Church. Records show that from the third century, a form of the current doxology was used at the conclusion of each psalm that was sung. This was true in both the eastern and western traditions.[48] The one problem that existed between East and West was that there was no common language in the doxologies used. This situation was rectified in 529 at the second Council of Vaison, which declared that all territories beyond the Alps must use the following invocation: "Glory be to the Father and to the Son and to the Holy Ghost, as it was in the beginning is now and ever shall be world without end. Amen."[49]

The association of the doxology with the rosary is a much later development considering the fact that the invocation had been used in church prayer since apostolic times. Although the doxology had been used with the psalms for centuries, its use with the prayers of the rosary was not popular until the dawn of the Renaissance. In a manuscript prayer book of the wealthy Danish widow Jesperdatter (circa 1500) there is a directive that the prayer of the Holy Trinity be added to every Our Father of the Psalter.[50] Here we see the first association of the doxology with the concept of the original *Na tri coicat* of *Paternosters*. Approximately fifty years later we see in a prayer book of Louis Blosius (died 1566) that one is directed to say the prayer of the Most Holy Trinity after each decade of Hail Marys. The prayer used was, "Praise be to the glorious Trinity, to the Father, the Son and the Comforter; praise be to the Virgin Mother of God, now and throughout eternity. Amen."[51] Although this form of the doxology is not consistent with that defined at Vaison, its use as a concluding prayer to a decade of Hail Marys in the Marian psalter is significant and a precursor to its actual use in the rosary of later years.

As strange as it might seem the doxology has never become a formally accepted prayer in the rosary. Its use, which as described above was common for several centuries, has never been incorporated as a particular prayer in the popular devotion. Some writers, agreeing with Father Thurston, credit the introduction of the trinitarian invocation at the end of each decade to the practice of the Dominican Church, Santa Maria Sopra Minerva at Rome.[52] Thurston bases this hypothesis on the description of the Sopra Minerva recitation of the rosary found in a book published by a Spanish Dominican at Madrid in 1613. According to this account, the rosary was chanted in imitation of vespers with five psalms. It began with the phrase, "O God come to my assistance," gave the mystery with a short meditation on it, and then inserted a preparatory antiphon. The Our Fathers and Hail Marys were then recited antiphonally, the two sides of the choir alternating. Each decade ended as did each psalm of the Office with the Gloria doxology.[53]

When Pope Leo XIII stated the essentials of the rosary in his first rosary encyclical, *Supremi Apostolatus* of September 1, 1883, there was no mention of the Gloria.[54] The Our Fathers and Hail Marys were specified and special emphasis was placed on the mysteries. Pope Pius XI in his encyclical *Ingravescentibus Malis* of September 29, 1937, describes the rosary as made up of the same three elements: "a magnificent crown woven with the angelical salutation, interlaced with the Lord's prayer, united to meditation, a most excellent form of prayer."[55] Although the doxology is not mentioned in either of these statements, common belief agrees with the statement of Father Thomas Esser who says that although the Gloria is not necessary for the gaining of the indulgences, "it is the most worthy and most fitting way of ending each decade."[56]

The Church's official definition of the rosary still remains that which was set down in the breviary for the Feast of the Most Holy Rosary: "The rosary is a certain form of prayer wherein we say fifteen decades of Hail Marys with an Our Father between each [decade], and recalling in pious meditation as many mysteries of our redemption as there are single [decades]."[57] The *Raccolta* of 1952 (the official English translation of *Enchiridion Indulgentiarum Preces et Pia Opera*, Vatican Press, 1950), which contains all "prayers and devotions enriched with indulgences in favor of all the faithful in Christ or of certain groups of persons," contains no other definition of the rosary.[58] Although the doxology is not officially proclaimed by the Church in its definition of the rosary, the prayer is universally used by the faithful in their daily recitation of this most popular of devotions.

Very little is known about the origins and associations of the Apostles' Creed and the *Salve Regina* with the rosary. Each prayer, however, has a rich derivation of its own. The Apostles' Creed is so named because medieval tradition ascribed the prayer to the twelve Apostles. According to the tradition, on the day of Pentecost, while under the direct inspiration of the Holy Spirit, the Apostles composed the prayer, each contributing one of the twelve articles contained therein.[59] This legend dates back to the sixth century and is foreshadowed even earlier by a sermon attributed to St. Ambrose.[60] Rufinus (circa 400) gives a detailed account of the prayer, assigning authorship to the Apostles as a joint effort, although not directly ascribing one article to each Apostle.[61] In a letter addressed to Pope Liberius by the Council of Milan (355) we have the first use of the phrase *Symbolum Apostolorum* (Creed of the Apostles) when describing the prayer. The letter states, "If you credit not the teachings of the priest . . . let credit at least be given to the Symbol of the Apostles which the Roman Church always preserves and maintains inviolate."[62]

Recent critics have assigned the origins of the Creed to a much later period than the apostolic age. Harnack, for example, asserts that in its present form, the Apostles' Creed represents only the baptismal confession of faith used in the Church of Southern Gaul in the latter fifth century.[63] In formal analysis Harnack's position is correct though Rome and not Gaul was the place of origin. The stress by Harnack on the lateness of the development does not seem to hold up to research, however. An older form of the Creed is known to exist in mid-second century Rome. Its differences from the present form are insignificant. Moreover, it is probable that the earlier Roman version, if not drawn up by the Apostles themselves, is at least based on an outline which dates back to the apostolic age.[64] Taking the prayer as a whole, we can confidently repeat the words of the twentieth century Protestant theologian Albert Zahm: "In and with our Creed we confess that which since the days of the Apostles has been the faith of united Christendom."[65]

The Creed makes its first appearance in the rosary as mentioned in the *Libellus Perutilis* published in 1495.[66] The author of this work suggests that the fifty Hail Marys with the *Paternosters* make a true garland of roses and points out that the Creed should be regarded as the hoop on which the whole construction is built. From this time forward the Apostles' Creed is commonly mentioned in association with rosary devotion. In the sixteenth century Cistercians became obliged to recite a Credo in addition to the Our Fathers and Hail Marys of the rosary.[67] Further evidence of this practice is found in *The Garden of Our Blessed Lady* by S. Chambers, S.J., published in 1612. Here the Creed is specifically mentioned as part of the pendant with three Hail Marys.[68]

The *Salve Regina*, or Hail Holy Queen, is the most celebrated of the four breviary anthems of the Blessed Virgin Mary. This prayer summarizes in appropriate medieval themes all the major Christian ideas about the Blessed Virgin. Mary is described as the mother chosen to replace Eve, the source of mercy, the advocate, the hope of eternal salvation and the embodiment of female tenderness. The *Salve Regina* entered into liturgical and popular prayer through the Latin church. It is found in twelfth century manuscripts as the Magnificat antiphon for the Feast of the Annunciation.[69] The Cistercian order used the prayer as a daily processional chant after 1218 and with compline from 1251; the

Dominicans and Franciscans adopted its use at about the same time.[70] In 1236 Pope Gregory IX ordered that it be chanted after compline on Fridays,[71] and from the fourteenth century it has been sung after compline universally in the Latin Rite.[72]

Authorship for this prayer is uncertain. Current historical research attributes it to Hermann ("the Cripple") Contractus (died 1054), although it has also been attributed to St. Bernard of Clairvaux, Peter of Compostela and Adhemar de Monteil of Puy (died 1002).[73] Composition in the eleventh or twelfth century seems most probable based on its aforementioned use with various religious communities.

Little is known of how the *Salve Regina* became a part of the rosary. It is probable that when Pope St. Pius V in 1568 decreed that the prayer be sung or recited after vespers from Trinity Sunday to the first Sunday in Advent,[74] that an association with the rosary was initiated. The timing with the official recognition of the rosary, following the Battle of Lepanto in 1571, seems very coincidental. By the seventeenth century the *Salve Regina*'s use in the rosary was almost universally accepted.[75]

The Mysteries

In discussing the repetitive nature of the prayers used in the rosary it could easily be misconstrued that the three "fifties" are part and parcel the bulk of this prayer. There can be no denying that as prayers go, the decades of *Aves* are the primary focus of the devotion. Much more central, however, to the whole message of the rosary is the series of mysteries and their retelling of the Jesus story. It is only natural that meditations on the life of Christ be the central focus of this devotion. As has been described previously, in moving from a recitation of fifty psalms to fifty *Paters* to fifty *Aves*, the devotion we now know as the rosary has placed Christ and his mother at the center of the history of salvation. Through the repetitious use of Hail Marys an atmosphere of meditation, analogous to that created in the Jesus prayer of eastern spirituality, is maintained for all who use the devotion.

Through the evolutionary history of the rosary the chief unifying element has been the mysteries and their meditation. The growth which the rosary achieved during the fifteenth century was promoted significantly by the use of mysteries to guide the recitation through the life of Jesus. The mysteries in many ways legitimized the rosary prayers, making them a meditation on the life of Jesus. Without a means of structuring meditative prayer on some theme, the rosary would have become an almost useless exercise of repeating words to complete the beads. The fifteenth century development of the mysteries, therefore, gives us the rosary as prayer, not merely repetitive words.

The first origins for the rosary mysteries can be attributed to Dominic of Prussia, a Carthusian monk living in the early fifteenth century.[76] The meditative element in prayer had always been present for religious in monastic life. As monks recited the psalms they would be thinking of the interpretation of the words. Thus these men would say one thing while thinking of another without expressing any conflict between the two. In his book *Liber Experientiarium*, Dominic composed a set of fifty clausulae (a brief summary statement of Christian belief), one for each *Ave* of the fifty. These mysteries were used as meditations while reciting the prayers aloud in a manner similar to the recitation of psalms in the Divine Office. The subject of these clausulae was the life of Jesus and his affiliation with Mary. The statements were similar to those found in Psalters of Jesus Christ and the Blessed Virgin Mary.

The fifty mysteries embraced the entire life of Jesus. Fourteen dealt with Jesus' hidden life; six dealt with his public life; twenty-two dealt with his passion and eight with Jesus' glorification and the coronation of Mary in heaven.[77] In order to alleviate many of the problems associated with memorizing so many mysteries, the clausulae were added to the original Hail Mary. The first Hail Mary, with its clause addition, read as follows: "Hail Mary, full of grace, the Lord is with thee. Blessed art thou among women, and blessed is the fruit of thy womb, Jesus, whom thou didst conceive by the Holy Spirit, through the message of an angel. Amen."[78] Dominic's final mystery read, ". . . who reigneth unconquered and glorious with the Father and the Holy Spirit and with thee, His glorious Mother, forever and ever. Amen."[79]

Mysteries and meditation came to the whole rosary by the expansion of the fifty clausulae of Dominic. People began fashioning garlands of praise for our Lady by putting together Hail Marys, Our Fathers, and "mysteries" in almost any arrangement that struck one's devotional fancy. St. Catherine of Bologna, a mid-fifteenth century Dominican nun (died 1463), composed a rosarium of verses, all incidents from the life of the Virgin Mary, that she used with each *Ave*.[80] A more modern looking form of meditation was introduced by Henry of Kalbar following the pattern of Dominic. Henry's use of fifty statements resulted in a rosary in which each Our Father was followed by ten Hail Marys, each with a mystery. This form comprised a series of five such decades, becoming popularized in the vernacular during the early sixteenth century from St. Gall in Switzerland.[81]

The natural progression which followed the work of Dominic and Henry of Kalbar was the expansion of the mysteries (clausulae) to 150, one for each *Ave* of the three fifties popular at this time. Many lists of 150 mysteries were generated during this period. Additionally, many rosary variations based on different numbers of mysteries began to become popular. Because such lists of various mysteries could not be memorized by most people, they were published in books from which the mysteries were read at each bead. This led to the common expression of "reading the rosary."[82]

The transition from 150 clausulae, one for each *Ave*, to the present fifteen mysteries begins with Alberto da Castello in the early sixteenth century. Published in 1521, his book *Rosario Della Gloriosa Vergine* uses the word mystery for the first time in association with the rosary.[83] This book also introduces the idea of having a mystery introduced by each *Paternoster*. The 150 clausulae are maintained but they are grouped so that ten can fall under each more generic mystery introduced at the outset of each decade.

Prior to the work of Alberto da Castello efforts were under

way to organize the mysteries into some coherent and logical pattern to simplify their memorization and enhance their use with the rosary. In 1483 an anonymous German Dominican priest published a Psalter in which he acknowledged a debt to Alanus de Rupe (who will be discussed in detail in the next chapter), while reducing the mysteries from 150 to fifteen, five joyful, five sorrowful and five glorious. The published book pictured the mysteries with a wreath of small roses representing the *Aves* and five dividing larger roses representing *Paternosters*.[84] Some scholars hypothesize that the division of the rosary into joyful, sorrowful and glorious mysteries can be traced back to the Marian Psalter of St. Bonaventure, *Psalter Immus Beatae Mariae Virgines*.[85] In this Psalter the first fifty stanzas begin with the word *ave*, the second fifty with the word *salve* and the third fifty with the word *gaude*. Other scholars claim that the division of the present fifteen mysteries can be traced back to Spain or Germany in the late fifteenth century.[86] This is based on artistic artifacts of the period. A Spanish woodcut dating from 1488 contains all fifteen of the present mysteries. Additionally, an altar piece from the church of a Dominican convent in Frankfurt, erected in 1490, contains all the present mysteries.

Although the precise origins of the modern fifteen mysteries and their division into three groups is not precisely known, we have references showing that three sets of five mysteries were in use by the turn of the sixteenth century. One of the original rosary books, *Unser Lieben Frauen Psalter*, has inserted in its center pages, three groups of five colored woodcuts representing the present joyful, sorrowful and glorious mysteries.[87] There is only one understandable exception: the Coronation of Mary (assimilated into the Assumption) is replaced by a meditation on the Last Judgment. The instructions for using the fifteen mysteries were as follows:

> These three pages with their pictures serve to show how you should say the psalter. On each page there are five pictures. If you want to say the psalter, look at the first picture before or while reciting the first ten *Aves*. When you have finished the first ten *Aves*, look at the second and recite the second ten *Aves*. Do the same for the third, fourth and fifth decades. You will then have finished with

the first page and its five pictures and with the first rosary and its five *Paters* and fifty *Aves*. The pictures on the second page are those of the second rosary and those on the third page those of the third rosary. Those are the ones you have to look at while saying the second and third rosaries.[88]

In 1573 at Rome the book *Rosario della Sacratissima* by A. Gianetti, O.P., set the modern fifteen mysteries in their typical division of joyful, sorrowful and glorious.[89] The mysteries had finally become the integral part of this meditative prayer.

Meditation on the mysteries of the rosary was championed by the Society of Jesus from the inception of the order. One influential book by Father Gaspard Loarte, S.J., published in 1573, gives much evidence of its content from its title, "Advice and Suggestions on the Manner of Meditating the Mysteries of the Rosary of the Blessed Virgin, Our Mother."[90] The influence of this work can be gauged by the rapidity with which translations appeared from French into German, Latin, Spanish and Portuguese. Its effect was so great on St. Aloysius of Gonzaga that it opened for him a new world of meditation.[91]

With some form of fifteen mysteries and their meditation in place, the stage was set for official Church recognition of the rosary. The sixteenth century and the pontificate of St. Pius V would prove to be the time when this recognition would come forth. Our story must, therefore, move to that century and the happenings therein.

Summary

The fifteenth century provided the development period for the many facets of today's rosary. During this period the Dominican influence with the rosary both grew and was fostered through fact and legend. Although many apocryphal accounts exist to explain how St. Dominic and his followers became originators of rosary devotion, it is evident that these accounts cannot stand up to the scrutiny of historical research. Although the Dominicans were not the sole originators of the rosary, their influence in the growth, devotion and spread of this prayer cannot be denied. It would not be inaccurate to call them the principal promoters and defenders of the rosary through history. This has been acknowledged by popes and scholars through the centuries. Certainly the fifteenth century was a period for much Dominican influence in this meditation, bringing a series of prayers and mysteries into a coherent form of prayer which today we all recognize as the rosary devotion.

The principal rosary developments of the fifteenth century were the definition of the individual prayers, plus the development of a series of mysteries which united this loosely connected series of prayers. The Hail Mary came to its present form through a two-step process. The first part of the prayer was a combination of the greetings of the angel Gabriel and Elizabeth to Mary as recorded by Luke the Evangelist. The exhortation in the prayer developed principally through the popular use of the laity. Only at the Council of Trent, however, did the Hail Mary receive the form commonly known today. The doxology (Glory be. . .) has roots in the Hebrew Scriptures and was commonly used by early Christians when reciting the psalms. Its addition to the prayers of the rosary follows the prayer's patterned use in the Apostolic and Patristic church. The Apostles' Creed and the *Salve Regina* are later additions to rosary devotion. Most probably composed by Hermann the Cripple in the eleventh century, the *Salve Regina* states all relevant medieval themes about the Blessed Virgin Mary. Although this is a most powerful and truly representative prayer of the period, it did not find its way into the rosary until the late sixteenth to early seventeenth century. It appears that the affiliation of the *Salve Regina* with the rosary came about through popular practice although its precise origin within the devotion is not known.

The mysteries of the rosary, the unifying glue to the devotion, came about through the introduction by Henry of Kalbar of fifty clausulae to be appended to each of the fifty *Aves*. Through a natural progression, the fifty clausulae expanded to 150, one for each *Ave* of the three "fifties." Development continued with the introduction of fifteen true mysteries, one for each *Paternoster*. The 150 clausulae were formed into groups of ten, corresponding to the fifteen mysteries. The use of clausulae gradually faded away, especially with the official recognition of the exhortation half of the Hail Mary. By 1573 there existed all the elements to form the present-day rosary including the fifteen contemporary mysteries. Our story will continue telling how the rosary became a recognized prayer of the Church.

Chapter 2 — Notes

1. Herbert Thurston, S.J., "Our Popular Devotions II: The Rosary VI, The Rise and Growth of the Dominican Tradition," *The Month* 97 (1901), p. 288.
2. *Ibid.*, p. 299.
3. *Ibid.*, p. 298.
4. Reginald Garrigou-Lagrange, O.P., "The Meaning of the Rosary," *Doctrine and Life* (October-November, 1952), p. 228.
5. *The Hours of the Divine Office in English and Latin*, vol. 3 (Collegeville, MN: The Liturgical Press), p. 1630.
6. Charles S. Dessain, ed., *The Letters and Diaries of John Henry Newman*, vol. 30 (Oxford: Clarendon Press, 1976), p. 232.
7. Pope Leo XIII speaks of St. Dominic's personal involvement with the rosary in *Supremi Apostolatus, Octobri mense, Magnae Dei Matris, Augustissimae Virginis, Laetitiae sanctae, Jucunda semper* and *Fidentem piumque*.
8. *Magnae Dei Matris*, encyclical letter of Pope Leo XIII, September 8, 1892, paragraph 8. See William Doheny, C.S.C., and Joseph Kelly, *Papal Documents on Mary* (Milwaukee: The Bruce Publishing Company, 1954), p. 69.
9. R. P. Devas, O.P., "The Rosary Tradition Defined and Defended," *American Catholic Quarterly Review* 41 (1916), p. 128.
10. Bede Jarrett, O.P., *The Life of Dominic* (Westminster, MD:

The Newman Bookshop, 1947), p. 110.

11. Idelfonso Cardinal Schuster, *Liber Sacramentorum, The Sacramentary* 5:9.

12. *Auchinleck Manuscript* in *A Penni Worth of Witte: Floric and Blancheflour; and Other Pieces of English Poetry,* ed. David Laing (Edinburgh: The Abbotsford Club, 1857).

13. Eithne Wilkins, *The Rose-Garden Game* (London: Victor Gollancz, LTD, 1969), p. 165.

14. Herbert Thurston, S.J., "Our Popular Devotions II: The Rosary I," *The Month* 96 (1900), p. 412.

15. Stephen Beissel, *Geschichte der Verehrung Marias in Deutschland Wahrend des Mittelalters,* vol. 1 (Freiburg: Herder & Company, 1909), p. 231.

16. K. Hofmann, "Ave Maria," *Lexikon fur Theologie und Kirche,* vol. 1, ed. Michael Buchberger (Freiburg: Herder & Company, 1930), p. 864.

17. Herbert Thurston, S.J., "Hail Mary," *Catholic Encyclopedia,* vol. 7 (New York: Robert Appleton, 1910), p. 111.

18. J. G. Shaw, *The Story of the Rosary* (Milwaukee: The Bruce Publishing Company, 1954), p. 36.

19. Jean Mabillon, *Annales Ordinis S. Benedicti Occidentalium Monachorum Patriarchae,* vol. 1, bk. 15, chap. 8 (Lucca: Leonardo Venturini, 1739), p. 422.

20. During the medieval period the "Little Office" of the Blessed Virgin Mary and other such Marian devotions became popular. It is probable that the greetings of Gabriel and Elizabeth began to be commonly joined at this time.

21. Beissel, *Geschichte der Verehrung Marias* 1:231.

22. Herbert Thurston, S.J., "Notes on Familiar Prayers I; The Origins of the Hail Mary," *The Month* 121 (1913), p. 173-74.

23. Franz Willam, *The Rosary: Its History and Meaning,* trans. Rev. Edwin Kaiser, C.P.P.S. (New York: Benziger Brothers, Inc., 1953), p. 21.

24. *Ibid.*

25. Thurston, "Hail Mary," p. 111.

26. *Ibid.* An indulgence for using the name of Jesus in the Hail Mary prayer was added by Pope John XXII (1316-1334).

27. *Ibid.,* pp. 111-12.

28. *Ibid.*
29. Thomas Esser, "Geschichte des Englischen Grusses, " in *Historisches Jahrbuch der Gorres Gesellschaft* (1884), p. 105.
30. The second letter of Cyril of Alexander to Nestorius was solemnly approved by the Council of Ephesus (431). In this letter Cyril defends the concept of Mary as the *Theotokos*, Godbearer. See Richard A. Norris, Jr., *The Christological Controversy* (Philadelphia: Fortress Press, 1980), pp. 131-35.
31. Shaw, *Rosary*, pp. 38-43.
32. The *Alma Redemptoris Mater* concludes with "have pity on sinners"; the *Ave Regina Coelorum* concludes with, "Pray to Christ for us."
33. Shaw, *Rosary*, pp. 38-43.
34. In his prayer book for the dying, St. Anselm concluded one prayer with the words, "Mary, Mother of grace, Mother of mercy, protect us against the evil spirit and take us to heaven at the hour of our death."
35. Shaw, *Rosary*, p. 43.
36. Hofmann, "Ave Maria," p. 864.
37. The petition used by the Camoldolese monks used the word "our" missing from Savonarola's prayer. It ended, ". . . now and at the hour of our death. Amen."
38. Willam, *The Rosary*, p. 86.
39. Shaw, *Rosary*, p. 44.
40. *Ibid.*
41. The Council of Trent, session 25, "Decree Concerning Reform," ordered the revision of the Roman catechism, missal and breviary. In the breviary the Hail Mary as we know it today was officially registered.
42. Shaw, *Rosary*, p. 44. In the post-Vatican II period this practice is rapidly dying out.
43. Thurston, "Hail Mary," p. 112.
44. Esser, "Geschichte des Englischen Grusses," p. 102.
45. See note 23.
46. Esser, "Geschichte des Englischen Grusses," p. 96.
47. Ludwig Eisenhofer, *Handbook of Catholic Liturgy*, vol. 1 (Freiburg: Herder & Herder, 1933), p. 169.
48. Wilkins, *Rose-Garden*, p. 69.

49. Eisenhofer, *Handbook*, p. 169.
50. Wilhelm Schmitz, S.J., *Das Rosenkranzgebet im 15 und am Angang des 16 Jahrhunderts* (Freiburg: Herder & Herder, 1903), p. 95.
51. Beissel, *Geschichte der Verehrung Marias*, p. 71.
52. See Thurston, "The Rosary," *Catholic Encyclopedia* 7:185, and Adrian Fortescue, "Doxology," *Catholic Encyclopedia* 5:151.
53. Shaw, *Rosary*, p. 107.
54. *Supremi Apostolatus* speaks of the origin, efficacy and devotion to the rosary. The latter speaks of the basic ten Hail Marys preceded by an Our Father. The Glory Be, however, is not mentioned.
55. *Ingravescentibus malis*, encyclical letter of Pope Pius XI, September 29, 1937, paragraph 16. See William Doheny and Joseph Kelly, *Papal Documents on Mary*, p. 182.
56. Shaw, *Rosary*, p. 109.
57. *The Hours of the Divine Office* 3:1633.
58. Joseph P. Christopher and Charles E. Spence, *The Raccolta* (New York: Benziger Brothers, Inc., 1944), pp. 270-73.
59. The Apostles' Creed when broken down into its component parts can be traced to twelve basic activities of faith (similar to the Nicene Creed) concerning God as Father, Son and Holy Spirit. See Herbert Thurston, S.J., "Apostles Creed," *Catholic Encyclopedia* 1:631. For a thorough historical description of the derivation see Nicholas Ayo, C.S.C., *Creed as Symbol* (Notre Dame: University of Notre Dame Press, 1989), pp. 9-18.
60. *Ibid.*, p. 629.
61. *Ibid.*
62. *Ibid.*
63. A. von Harnack, *Das Apostolische Glaubenskbekenntsniss* (1892), p. 3.
64. Thurston, "Apostles Creed," p. 630.
65. *Ibid.*
66. Shaw, *Rosary*, p. 103.
67. See Hugo Sejalon, ed., *Nomasticon Cisterciense* part of *Usus Conversorum* (Solesmes, 1892), p. 234.

68. Shaw, *Rosary*, p. 104.
69. R. J. Snow, "Salve Regina," *New Catholic Encyclopedia*, vol. 12 (New York: McGraw-Hill Book Company, 1967), p. 1002.
70. *Ibid.*
71. *Ibid.*
72. *Ibid.*
73. *Ibid.*
74. *Ibid.*
75. With the official recognition of the rosary by Pope St. Pius V the prayer began to be formalized and the various versions began to condense into the now familiar contemporary format. The *Salve Regina* or Hail Holy Queen became a formal rosary prayer as a result of this format.
76. Wilkins, *Rose-Garden*, p. 40.
77. Beissel, *Geschichte der Verehrung Marias*, p. 515.
78. *Ibid.*
79. *Ibid.*
80. Wilkins, *Rose-Garden*, p. 107.
81. Beissel, *Geschichte der Verehrung Marias*, p. 518.
82. The expression "reading the rosary" was a natural outgrowth of the many books that contained versions of 150 clausulae. People would use the books more than the beads since one could keep track of the prayers by following along in the book.
83. Herbert Thurston, S.J., "Our Popular Devotions: The Rosary 111; Fifteen Mysteries," *The Month* 96 (1900), p. 629.
84. Wilkins, *Rose-Garden*, p. 72.
85. Shaw, *Rosary*, p. 28.
86. This hypothesis is supported principally by artistic evidence in Spain and Germany that shows the mysteries in their present configuration.
87. Thurston, "The Fifteen Mysteries," p. 624.
88. *Ibid.*, pp. 625-27.
89. *Ibid.*, p. 630.
90. Shaw, *Rosary*, p. 102.
91. Alban Butler, *Lives of the Saints*, vol. 6, edited and revised by Herbert Thurston, S.J. and Norah Leeson (London: Burns, Oates & Washbourne, LTD, 1937), pp. 270-71.

Chapter 3
Church Recognition

Our story of the rosary has brought together a series of prayers and meditations which were counted on beads, knotted cord or some similar counting device. The organization of these prayers and mysteries plus their recognition in the Church as an established form of prayer devotion is the next step in this exposition of the rosary's development. This chapter aims at describing the primarily sixteenth century development of the rosary, a period which took this devotion from a composite of prayers and forms to a rosary which was, according to the hierarchical Church, universally accepted.

As has been previously described, the story of the rosary is very much entwined with the evolutionary history of prayer. Once the basic prayers and mysteries had been brought together, it still remained for the form of the prayers to be established. Numerous forms of rosaries, usually altering the number of *Aves* and *Paters*, sprang up in the fifteenth through seventeenth centuries.[1] Each version of the prayer was initiated for a specific devotion or used by a specific community of people, either geographically or by religious congregation. In the latter sixteenth century, however, the Church acted to officially recognize the rosary, giving to the prayer an approved form.

This form, adopted in 1573, is the standard in use today. Although some aberrations of this standard fifteen decade, 150 *Ave* rosary are still found, they are mostly limited to special applications in religious communities where they have been used possibly for centuries.

The Rosary Takes Shape

How the rosary evolved to its present form is a most interesting saga. Our story must begin with the formation of decades of Hail Marys preceded by an Our Father. Precisely how and when the Our Father and Hail Mary came together in one rosary is only speculation. Several theories have been put forth to answer this question. Archeological evidence shows rosary beads separated in groups of ten with a large bead as a marker.[2] It is possible that the large bead was used for an Our Father after ten *Aves*. It is equally likely, however, that the large bead was present for counting and that the Our Father came into use *because* of the large bead rather than the bead for the Our Father. This "marker" theory is supported by an incised slab bearing a representation of Marguerite de Chatelvain carrying a long rosary which is divided by larger beads into groups of five.[3] Additionally, we find the name *marker* applied to the larger beads in several testaments and inventories.[4] In his study "The Collection of Rosaries in the United States National Museum," Immanuel M. Casanowicz notes some instances of this understanding. "In the inventory of the plate and jewels of Charles V, King of France in 1380, there are enumerated nineteen rosaries made of rose-tinted amber and jet coral with pearls for markers. So again in the inventory of the Princess of Orleans, Valois, in 1408, there are entered a rosary of amethysts and jasper with a stud of pearls, another of jet with nine little bells of gold and a jewel with nine pearls as pendant, and another again of jet with nine gold markers and a gold figurine of St. Christopher attached."[5]

Other themes on the unification of the Our Father and the Hail Mary in the rosary circulate through the literature. Twentieth century scholar Canon Willam has suggested that any rosary development beyond the fourteenth century was based on various adaptations of the Psalter. He hypothesizes that the rosary developed from the union of four Psalters, the Psalter of 150 Our Fathers, the Psalter of 150 Hail Marys, the Jesus Psalter of 150 psalms and the Marian Psalter of psalms interpreted as mirrors or prefigurements of Mary.[6] The Psalter of *Aves* and *Paters* ultimately developed into the present sequence of prayers in individual decades. The second two Psalters developed the mysteries and meditation. The so-called Rule of Baumberg (twelfth century) states that *Aves* should be added to each *Paternoster* of the Psalter, alternating one for another.[7]

Once an association between *Aves* and *Paternosters* was made, the next step was to structure their order for use within the prayer. The custom of separating or really originating each decade of *Aves* with an Our Father stems from the fourteenth century forward. Much of the work in this area must be attributed to the Carthusian tradition. The Hail Mary appears in official Carthusian records beginning in 1233.[8] The addition of the Our Father to each of fifteen decades is attributed to Henry Egher (Henry of Kalbar who we met in the last chapter in association with the mysteries), visitator of the order, who died in 1408.[9] The Hail Marys of the Marian Psalter were bracketed into decades with fifteen Our Fathers standing like columns between the Hail Marys. The archives of the Rhine province of the Carthusian order relate a story of how Mary instructed Henry in the ordering of the prayers. Mary told him that a more perfect Psalter could be constructed by "first of all saying one *Paternoster* and ten *Ave Marias*, again one *Paternoster* and ten *Ave Marias* and so on until you have completed 15 *Paters* and 150 *Aves*."[10]

English influence in the development of the decades was very pronounced. Through Carthusian practice the concept of using *Paters* with each decade of *Aves* came to England. Records show that in 1440 students of Eton College were required to daily recite the Psalter of the Blessed Virgin Mary, consisting of fifteen Our Fathers and 150 Hail Marys.[11] Herbert Thurston has written, "at the close of the 14th century and the beginning of the 15th century we hear more about the rosary from England than anywhere else. And the form of Our Lady's Psalter in which *Aves* are divided into decades by *Paters* seems first of all to have been general in England."[12]

The rosary pendant, prayed as a preparation for the decades and mysteries, has a much later origin. General historical evidence seems to indicate that the pendant consisting of the Apostles' Creed, Our Father and three Hail Marys came to the contemporary rosary via the six decade, sixty-three Hail Mary rosary popular in the sixteenth and seventeenth centuries.[13] (These alternate rosary forms will be detailed in the following paragraphs.) *The Garden of Our Blessed* Lady by Father S. Chambers, S.J., published in 1612, gives a history of the pendant accompanied by either five or six decades of Aves.[14] In the *Sacri Rosarii Excercitationes* published by Father Guy Bourgesuis, S.J., at Antwerp in 1622, references are found to the pendant and the six decade corona: "Our ancestors were not satisfied with constantly reciting the Psalter and the rosary of the Mother of God, but they added to this the corona which was intended to commemorate in one round of the beads all the years spent by Our Lord or his Mother in this mortal life." He further states that the corona consisted of six decades with three *Ave* beads added to make up the number sixty-three, the reputed number of years spent by Mary on earth.[15]

Various rosary forms, both in number of beads and prayers as well as mysteries continued to be prevalent up to the middle of the sixteenth century. A distinction must be made here in terms. Any form of "rosary" devotion other than one with five, ten or fifteen decades is not truly a rosary but a chaplet or corona. Many Roman Catholic religious communities have a corona of their own in addition to the standard five-decade rosary.[16] The Middle Ages produced many variations in chaplets. The Teutonic Knights and the Knights of St. John wore beads in their sword belts as a sort of *parte-epee*.[17] Three forms now forgotten from this period include one with beads in octaves, one with thirty beads held together as an open string or as a chaplet and one of groups of twelve *Aves* based on the number of stars in our Lady's crown as described in the Book of Revelation.[18] Both of the latter appear in fifteenth century paintings.[19] Other prevalent forms of coronas were a chaplet of thirty-three *Aves*, representing the thirty-three years of

Jesus' life and one with ninety-six *Aves*, representing the thirty-three years of Jesus' life and the purported sixty-three years of Mary's life.[20]

Away from the mainstream development of the rosary many versions of similar devotion continued to flourish well into the nineteenth century. The Brigettine corona (based on the revelation to St. Bridget of Sweden), as mentioned earlier in its affiliation with the rosary pendant, contained sixty-three Hail Marys, one for each year of Mary's life.[21] The prayer form did not exist during Bridget's life (1304-1373) but was brought to prominence based on her revelations which were held in high esteem and widely read after her death. The chaplet of the Seven Dolors was constructed of seven groups of seven *Aves* to commemorate the sorrows of Mary: (1) the prophecy of Simeon, (2) the flight to Egypt, (3) the loss of the twelve-year-old Jesus, (4) Mary meeting Jesus on the Via Dolorosa, (5) the hours spent beneath the cross, (6) the resting of the dead Jesus in his mother's arms, and (7) the laying of Jesus in the tomb. This chaplet was later joined with an additional three Hail Marys to be said for the tears shed by our Lady during her sorrows.[22]

An interesting survivor of the medieval and Renaissance proliferation of chaplets is a rosary still used in the village of Schrocken in the Alps. This rosary has sixty-three Hail Marys but is devoid of Our Fathers. Each Hail Mary contains a relative clause dependent upon the name of Jesus. Only the original biblical portion of the prayer is recited.[23] The number of Hail Marys shows the influence of the Brigettine corona and the form in which meditation is inserted in each follows the custom introduced by the Carthusian rosary of Dominic the Prussian. The clausulae, constituting the sixty-three mysteries of the Schrocken rosary, are read aloud by a reader as the congregation reaches the end of each Hail Mary. The final three clausulae said after the pendant Hail Marys (reversing the order of contemporary rosary recitations) give the flavor of the whole prayer: (1) Grant that we may hear with devotion the word of God, (2) Grant that we may keep the word of God in our hearts, and (3) Grant that we may attain the happiness of heaven through Jesus Christ.[24]

The Rosary Confraternity

The mid-fifteenth century was the historical period which placed the rosary in the hands of all by its recognition within the Church. As we have previously discussed, all the necessary parts of the rosary puzzle were present by this time. Prayers, mysteries and even a basically sound structure of decades was in place. The principal obstacle to overcome in rosary devotion was its individuality. Seldom, if ever, was the rosary a form of communal prayer; its scope was limited to the individual. Lack of formal recognition of the rosary by any established Church organization kept this prayer on a path to extinction. This was not to be the fate of the rosary, however, through the arduous work of various religious groups, especially the Dominicans and Carthusians. As has been previously described, the Dominicans continued to play a significant role in promoting devotion to the rosary, even if the stories of Mary and St. Dominic are apocryphal. The Carthusians were principally responsible for structuring the prayers and for the promotion of the work of Henry of Kalbar. The major figure of this era, in the promotion of the rosary, however, was another Dominican, Blessed Alanus de Rupe and his Confraternity of the Rosary.

Although rare, some organizations for promotion of rosary devotion did exist prior to the fifteenth century. Two Dominican groups were especially noteworthy. The Militia of Christ (founded by St. Dominic) and the Confraternity of Prayer (founded in 1259) promoted the rosary as it then existed.[25] The main problem, however, was that there really was no rosary to promote. As we recall, the thirteenth century had the various Psalters; some early form of the devotion may have even existed on beads. But the mysteries, the central part of the rosary, were not in use at this time. Therefore, although acting as forerunners for the Rosary Confraternity, these groups could not be sustained at the time.

In Alanus de Rupe and the Confraternity of the Rosary which he founded in 1470 we undoubtedly have the greatest single influence in the formation of the rosary as it exists today. This influence, however, did not take the form of an already perfected rosary brought intact to the whole Christian world. The Confraternity did, however, provide the organization which, in a remarkably short time, brought general unity to a previously scrambled group of prayers and meditations. But in the beginning, while adhering to a basic pattern which ultimately produced conformity, there still existed a significant plurality of rosary forms which the evolutionary nature of this devotion had generated.

From the historical record it is evident that more than any other person Alanus de Rupe, a Breton Dominican, deserves the title of "Father of the Rosary." He was born in Brittany in 1428 and was renowned by people of his period for his holiness, learning and zeal. He held high positions in the Dominicans, including the post of Visitor to the Dominicans of Poland.[26] He is honored in the order and the Church as Blessed Alanus. Despite the positive reputation which preceded him, scholars today wonder at his effectiveness, citing his highly exaggerated and historically inaccurate statements and claims. The unsubstantiated statement of St. Dominic's role as originator of the rosary is only one of many statements that were conjured up out of thin air. A perfect example of this is his bizarre statement that God and Mary had given indulgences in excess of 60,000 years for faithful recitation of Our Lady's Psalter![27] These statements seem somewhat ridiculous to our ears but for the people of fifteenth century Europe they may have been the catalyst necessary to promote the rosary to universal acceptance and use.

Alanus first founded the Confraternity at Douai in northern France in the year 1470 under the title, "Confraternity of the Psalter of Jesus and Mary."[28] The previously founded associations, mentioned above, to promote pious recitation of the rosary, were not designed to achieve universal recognition. Alanus' aim in founding the Confraternity was to bring all such previously formed groups into one organization centered at Rome. Alanus was not able to accomplish this task personally; the Confraternity was not approved by Rome, thinking it inappropriate to universally recognize a seemingly purely Dominican activity. Papal approval did come, however, five years later on September 8, 1475, the date of Alanus de Rupe's death. Approval was granted to a confraternity, based on de Rupe's model, that was organized by Jacob Sprenger, O.P., at Cologne.[29]

The Confraternity did not take long to prove its popularity. In the first four months of its existence at Cologne, 5,000 names were inscribed in the official register. By the end of the next year (1476), there were 50,000 enrolled.[30] Michael Francisci, an associate of Alanus de Rupe, writing in 1479 said that there were then 500,000 names on file, "and the register will contain yet more names, for it is growing and spreading from day to day throughout different provinces, cities and places."[31] A succession of popes beginning with Sixtus IV granted indulgences and privileges to the associates of the Confraternity.[32] Each new recognition from Rome gave renewed impetus to the movement that was fast gathering all devotees to Mary's Psalter into a single fold.

A very important element to the spread of the Confraternity was the simplicity and leniency of its requirements as drawn up by the genius of Alanus. In the first place there was no question of fees. Indulgences were attached; deceased relatives and friends could be enrolled. The two basic obligations were recitation of Our Lady's Psalter once a week and reception of Holy Communion on the first Sunday of the month.[33] One simply entered one's name on the register, fulfilled the two simple requirements and one "belonged." One became a member of an officially recognized society of the universal Church. This might not seem like such a big prize for us today when such universal church associations are plentiful. During the fifteenth century, however, when geographical isolation and lack of communication made worldwide unions rare and precious, being a member of the Rosary Confraternity was an important and honored position. With the societal conditions as such, it is not surprising at all that the "Dominican Rosary" adopted by the Confraternity was the form which prevailed and became the standard for the universal Church.

Speculation exists as to what Alanus meant in his Confraternity rule that "Our Lady's Psalter must be said once per week." Evidence from his aforementioned unusual writings and from those who followed him shows that a certain cycle of meditation on the Psalter was needed. Also, it is generally thought that Alanus meant a Psalter of fifty *Aves* and five *Paters*, although there is still much conjecture on this issue.[34] In investigating the first manuals of the Confraternity to learn what the members were actually supposed to say, we find the same lack of definition, although the general flavor of the "Dominican Rosary" continues to dominate.[35]

The first printed manual of the Confraternity was written by Jacob Sprenger, O.P., founder of the Cologne organization, and published in 1476. The book has no title but begins with this appropriate Latin admonition: "*In Spiritu Penses Hoc Opus Nec Litteram Spectes*"; ponder this book in the Spirit and do not look to the letter. The text states that Confraternity members must say each week three rosaries (adding to the basic requirement of Alanus de Rupe), making one complete Psalter of fifteen *Paters* and 150 *Aves*. Although no specific practice of meditation is prescribed, the members are told that "after ten white roses, they must insert one red rose, symbolized by the Paternoster, in which we reflect upon the rose-red blood of Jesus Christ, which God Our Father has willed to be shed for our sakes."[36]

A second book, the aforementioned (in chapter 3) *Unser Lieben Frauen Psalter*, published in 1489, attained a very wide circulation. It is historically important for its use of the fifteen mysteries and became a precursor to the "Rosary Picture Books" which became very popular. The book announces that its contents are "taken out of a little book made by Master Alanus, of the Order of Preachers, concerning Our Lady's Psalter."[37] The text explains how Mary's Psalter is to be said, using the three sets of fifty *Aves* as was common at that time. The main treasures of the book for the historian of the rosary, however, are the three pages in the center and the instructions for their use. Each of these three pages shows a group of five colored woodcuts which represent with one exception the present-day fifteen mysteries of our present rosary. Each of the individual pictures is enclosed in a garland of roses in which groups of ten smaller roses are separated by one larger rose. Despite the fact that the Dominican rosary was certainly the major emphasis of this work, other rosaries are mentioned by the author, including one of 150 Aves with a meditation on each. The author concludes by saying, "Thus [by uniting vocal prayer with meditation] you can arrange the Psalter of Mary in one manner or the other, if it pleases you."[38]

The most successful rosary picture book that bore the mark of the Confraternity was the aforementioned *Rosario Della Gloriosa Vergine* by Alberto da Castello, O.P., first printed at Venice in 1521.[39] In this book every one of the 150 Hail Marys has a separate picture engraved for it, representing a different aspect of the mystery in which it belongs. Although the presentation of the book must have been costly, a number of editions were printed. The book is especially significant in its transition from the old 150 mysteries, to which the laity clung, to the new fifteen mysteries, toward which some people were tending. The book's format allowed the new method to become habit without any sense of disloyalty to the old method.

Father da Castello's work, originally published in Italian with additional editions, appeared in French at Paris in 1579 and in German at Mainz in 1599. The combination of the old and new together with the effect of other "Rosary Picture Books" established the strong position of the Dominican rosary by putting in the hands of Confraternity members local handbooks which emphasized the now familiar arrangement of the fifteen mysteries.

Although other religious communities assisted in the development and promotion of the rosary, the influence of the Dominicans and their Rosary Confraternity cannot be overemphasized. We have already seen something of the Carthusian contribution at a critical point in the history of the rosary. The Jesuit influence was considerable, especially upon the form of the mysteries. Canon Willam has put forth a most apt and figurative comparison for Dominican and Jesuit influence on the mysteries. He says that for the Dominicans the rosary was a Marian church with its fifteen mysteries standing as altars before which one proclaimed Mary's glory and implored her intercession for the faithful. For the Jesuits, on the other hand, the rosary was an exercise hall in which one proposed to the faithful fifteen points of meditation, easily understood through pictures, while praying for grace to conform their lives to the examples given in the mysteries.[40] The Dominican

Rosary Confraternity advanced the rosary through its popular appeal, ease of membership and promotion of a standard form of prayer. Through the work of the Confraternity, its books and those texts influenced by it, we can understand how the Dominican form of the rosary became the standard recognized by Rome in the latter sixteenth century.

Official Church Recognition

The second half of the sixteenth century saw the Rosary Confraternity's work crowned by official recognition of the rosary in the liturgical life of the Church. In less than 100 years after the death of Alanus de Rupe, his Confraternity had brought about the establishment of the Feast of the Most Holy Rosary. In October 1474, the city of Cologne was miraculously saved from attack by Burgundian troops. This victory was attributed to the rosary by Jacob Sprenger, the Dominican prior of the city and founder of the Cologne Confraternity, who had asked that the Psalter of Our Lady be prayed to bring victory. The victory by Don Juan of Austria in a naval battle against the Turks at Lepanto on the first Sunday of October 1571, was also attributed to the rosary. On the same day of the Lepanto battle, the Rosary Confraternities of Rome had held processions which so coincided with the important victory that Pope St. Pius V declared that from that time forward a commemoration of the rosary would be made in the Mass for that day. In *Salvatoris Domini*, March 5, 1572, St. Pius stated, "We desire in particular that the remembrance of the great victory obtained from God through the merits and intercession of the glorious Virgin, on October 7, 1571, against the Turks, the enemies of the Catholic Faith, may never be forgotten."[41] In his decree the pope granted indulgences to the faithful who would remember in prayer the victory at Lepanto:

> Furthermore, trusting in the mercy of almighty God and in the authority of the blessed Apostles Peter and Paul, we mercifully grant in the Lord and bestow for the present and in perpetuity:
> —to each and every member of this Confraternity, present and to come, as well as to the other faithful, who are truly repentant,

have confessed their sins, and have been strengthened, fortified with the sacraments of the Church,

—who, on the day of the feast of the Blessed Virgin Mary of the Rosary which from now on should be celebrated each year on October 7 (instead of on the second Sunday in May), and which we transfer in perpetuity to the date of October 7, in memory of the victory of which we have spoken above and in honor of the Blessed Virgin

—shall devoutly visit the chapel of these confraternities, and there, will pray in remembrance of this victory, for the spread of the Catholic Faith and the extirpation of heresies, a plenary indulgence *toties quoties* (each time), and the remission of their sins.[42]

In 1573, at the request of the Dominican Order, Pope Gregory XIII established the Feast of the Most Holy Rosary. This was celebrated on the first Sunday of October, originally October 7, celebrating the victory at Lepanto. Initially the feast was granted only to churches which had an altar dedicated to the rosary. In 1671 Pope Clement X extended observance of the feast to all of Spain. Another victory over the Turks, this time at Peterwardein in Hungary by Prince Eugene on the Feast of our Lady of the Snows, August 5, 1716, led Pope Clement XI to extend the Feast of the Holy Rosary to the universal Church. The Church's official definition of the rosary was set down in the breviary for the feast originally established by Pope Gregory XIII. Although the rosary had become officially recognized, the prayer we say today continues to display an evolutionary process similar to which this book has described in detail.

In the Mass for any feast we always find an unexcelled distillation of the Church's thought on the person, event or devotion being celebrated. Such is the case for the Mass of the Feast of the Most Holy Rosary. Under the 1969 reconstruction of the liturgical calendar this feast is celebrated as an obligatory memorial for the universal Church.[43] Reflection on the prayers for the Mass show the clear mind of the Church in celebrating this devotion. The opening prayer reveals the life, death and resurrection of Christ, central mysteries of the rosary: "Lord, fill our hearts with your love, and as you revealed to us by an angel the coming of your Son as man, so lead us through his suffering and death to the glory of his resurrection. . ."[44] The prayer over the gifts is even more illustrative of the nature of the mystery of Christ: "By celebrating the mysteries of your Son, may we become worthy of the eternal life of promises. . ."[45] The entrance antiphon for this feast shows both the biblical and historical roots of this devotion in the construction of the Hail Mary: "Hail Mary, full of grace, the Lord is with you; blessed are you among women and blessed is the fruit of your womb."[46]

The Mass of the Feast of the Most Holy Rosary written in the sixteenth century is even more descriptive of the significance of this day. In the collect we read,". . . we pray, that in meditating upon these mysteries in the most holy rosary of the Blessed Virgin Mary, we may initiate what they contain and obtain what they promise."[47] The offertory verse recalls the rose garden and its association with the prayer: "In me is all grace of the way and the truth; in me is all hope of life and of virtue. As a rose planted by the running waters have I budded forth."[48] The secret brings us back from a consideration of the person of Mary to the particular method by which she and her Son are being honored: "Make us worthy, O Lord, to offer these gifts to thee, and through the mysteries of the Most Holy Rosary, make us so to keep in mind the life, passion and glory of thy only begotten Son, that we may be made worthy of his promises."[49] The postcommunion prayer re-presents the idea of the rosary mysteries: "May we find aid, O Lord, we beg thee, in the prayers of thy most holy mother, whose rosary we are celebrating, that we may draw strength from the mysteries which we reverence and gain the effect of the sacraments which we have received."[50]

Rosary Devotion — St. Louis de Montfort

As has been described, the first limited granting of the Feast of the Most Holy Rosary was made in 1573. The feast was extended to the universal Church in 1716. Between these two dates, the rosary we have today came into general usage in its essentially complete and definitive form. Variations, as we have seen, continued to exist, but these differences add little, save incidental interest, to the history of this devotion. Before the story of the historical derivation of the rosary is closed, however, it is important to trace the development of this prayer in the popular devotion of the faithful.

Fortunately for us the task of gathering information on the popular devotion of the rosary is relatively simple. From the sixteenth century forward the Dominican rosary became such an integral part of the Church's life of prayer that the historian can pick up the tale at virtually any step along the way. One can produce a chronological succession of papal statements and diocesan directives which testify to the rosary's universal practice. Additionally, many religious communities taught the Dominican rosary form, even if they encouraged the practice of some other corona or chaplet. Best of all, one can examine the devotional practice and/or writings of virtually any saint of that period and come in contact with the rosary. If a work existed which gave proof of the rosary's general acceptance at that time, while simultaneously exposing the meaning, purpose and excellence of the prayer today, then we would have a fitting conclusion to this outline of the historical development of this prayer.

Fortunately there is a book excellently suited to this need. *The Secret of the Most Holy Rosary*, written by St. Louis Marie de Montfort, gives us much insight into the popular rosary devotion of the seventeenth century. St. Louis, who died in 1716, the year of universal acceptance of the rosary feast, wrote his book based upon the Dominican Rosary Confraternity book published in 1680.[51]

The Secret of the Most Holy Rosary is valuable both as a link in the historical chain and as a manual for the prayer's recitation. The book stays true to the Confraternity tradition and the writings of Alanus de Rupe attributing the rosary to St. Dominic.[52] Although, as we have seen, this conclusion is not historically accurate, as a piece of historical evidence the book does prove three things: (1) the rosary taught by St. Louis de Montfort was the very rosary we have today, (2) devotion to the rosary had become so common that the prayer was looked upon as the badge of a Catholic, and (3) the rosary had been and was being extolled and recommended by other spiritual leaders in many nations.[53]

The rosary mentioned by St. Louis, in its completeness, bridges gaps in the historical evolution of the prayer and gives us a date at which we may consider the development of the rosary to be complete. The rosary described begins with the Creed, followed by one Our Father and three Hail Marys. It has fifteen decades of Hail Marys, with one Our Father and one Glory Be added to each. The decades accompany meditations on the fifteen mysteries as we have them today. Everything as we know it (save the angel's prayer from Fatima) is present.[54] This is particularly noteworthy since, as has been described, numerous variations existed and the use of the rosary pendant and Glory Be were far from standard practices.

Although not as true today, the rosary has been the badge for Catholics for many years. St. Louis takes it for granted that all Catholics know the rosary and its method of recitation. For him it is a distinguishing mark separating practicing from nonpracticing Catholics. St. Louis writes, "My *Ave Maria*, my rosary (or my chaplet), is my prayer and my most certain touchstone for distinguishing between those who are guided by the Spirit of God and those who work under the illusion of the evil spirit."[55] The rosary as a badge of Catholicism is still evident but not as St. Louis has described. If a person injured in some mishap were to have a rosary in their possession it would be natural to call a priest assuming that the person is Catholic. Additionally, it is not unusual to see rosaries dangling from the rear view mirrors of cars, a clear sign that the owner is Catholic.

Throughout the rest of his book St. Louis mentions many saints from throughout Europe who have expressed support for the spread of rosary devotion. Among the many people mentioned are St. Robert Bellarmine, St. Francis de Sales, St. Charles Borromeo, St. Ignatius Loyola, St. Teresa of Avila and St. Philip Neri.[56] These people are representative of the sixteenth and seventeenth centuries, covering the period from the rise of the Rosary Confraternity to de Montfort himself. However casual and incomplete is his evidence of the rosary's prevalence outside France, he leaves no doubt by referring to several canonized people of the era that rosary devotion was strong in the universal Church.

St. Louis' exposition of the rosary and its use is highlighted by the four introductions he uses in the book.[57] The devotion is placed in proper order — the worship of God comes first; the rosary, like all devotions to Mary and like our Lady herself, is significant only as a means to that end. De Montfort's concept of the rosary as prayer ultimately directed to God places its efficacy within the realm of all people, the mighty, the lowly, the saint and the sinner, the theologian and the uneducated. The use of four separate introductions, one to priests, one to sinners, one to devout souls and one to little children, makes it quite clear that he intended his book for all these peoples.

Although designed for diverse groups, the introductions show the rosary's direction toward God. In his first introduction, "A White Rose for priests," we read, "We ought to pattern ourselves on Our Blessed Lord, who began by practicing what he preached. We ought to emulate St. Paul who knew and preached nothing but Jesus crucified. This is really and truly what you will be doing if you preach the Holy Rosary."[58] The second introduction continues on this theme: "Poor men and women who are sinners, I, a greater sinner than you, wish to give to you this rose — a crimson one, because the Precious Blood of Our Lord has fallen upon it."[59] The last two introductions of de Montfort's work combine ideas of worship of Jesus and veneration of Mary. In the third introduction we read, "Of course you understand what I mean, since you are spiritually-minded; this mystical rose tree is Jesus and Mary in life, death and eternity. . ."[60] In his introduction to children St. Louis states, "This rosary will be your little wreath of roses, your crown for Jesus and Mary."[61] In a fitting manner to honor Jesus and Mary, St. Louis closes the introduction as follows: "Therefore let all men, the learned and the ignorant, the just and the sinner, the great and the small praise and honor Jesus and Mary night and day by saying the Most Holy Rosary."[62]

The body of the book is divided into two parts — "What the

Rosary Is" and "How to Recite It." There are four divisions to the first part. They deal with the origin and name of the rosary, the prayers of which it is composed, the meditations, and a recounting of wonderful favors received through its power. The second part speaks of the dispositions one should bring to the recitation of the rosary, and it gives several methods of praying it.

There is little out of the ordinary in what St. Louis has to say about any of these things. He draws largely on the early handbooks of the Rosary Confraternity and quotes them frequently.[63] The extraordinary thing about the book is that it is so true to the rosary teaching of today that it sounds proper and ordinary to our ears. Out of the volumes written about the rosary before his time, out of the variety of approaches to it, de Montfort unerringly hit dead center on the permanent essentials of the devotion.

Throughout *The Secret of the Rosary*, de Montfort stresses the efficacy of the rosary in daily life. In the twenty-seventh rose of the book he summarizes the benefits of the rosary:

1. It gradually gives us a perfect knowledge of Jesus Christ.
2. It purifies our souls, washing away sin.
3. It gives us victory over all enemies.
4. It makes it easy for us to practice virtue.
5. It sets us on fire with love of Our Blessed Lord.
6. It enriches us with graces and merits.
7. It supplies us with what is needed to pay all our debts to God and to our fellow men, and finally, it obtains all kinds of graces for us from Almighty God.[64]

In *The Secret of the Rosary* St. Louis de Montfort has provided the link between past and present in devotion to the rosary. Through a unique combination detailing some of the evolutionary history of the rosary and its meaning for future generations, St. Louis has provided us with a remarkable document that is amazing for its relevance more than 250 years after its publication. By using the Dominican rosary of 1680, St. Louis has remarkably composed a style of rosary recitation that basically finalized the prayer's evolutionary development. With one slight exception (the angel's prayer of Fatima, and that event did not occur until 1917), the rosary described by St. Louis is that used by the Roman Catholic faithful of today. The composition of *The Secret of the Rosary* is highly significant for rosary devotion as we know it today.

Summary

During the sixteenth century the rosary began to take the shape we have today, leading to its official recognition in 1571. At the dawn of the fifteenth century, the prayers and mysteries of the rosary were fairly well defined. During this period and into the sixteenth century the ordering of the prayers and mysteries into a contemporarily recognizable rosary format took place. Different theories exist as to how the association of *Aves* and *Paters* in the same decade came about. Archeological evidence shows "marker" beads existed separating the *Aves* from each other. It is possible that these "marker" beads were used for recitation of *Paternosters*. Canon Willam has hypothesized that the association came through some joining of the Psalters of 150 *Aves* and 150 *Paters*. Ordering of these prayers was greatly influenced by the Carthusian Order and especially by Henry of Kalbar. The rosary pendant was a later development, being added to the rosary only in the early seventeenth century.

The fourteenth century and beyond saw many different versions of the rosary. These variations were principally in the number of *Aves* and *Paters* used rather than in their ordering. Three of the most noteworthy of these rosary coronas were the Brigettine corona, the chaplet of the Seven Dolors and the Schrocken rosary.

The most significant event in the historical derivation of the rosary was the formation of the Rosary Confraternity by Blessed Alanus de Rupe in the latter fifteenth century. Individuality, the principal obstacle restricting rosary devotion, was erased by the Confraternity. The communal and thus conforming attitude that the Confraternity put forth raised the whole consciousness of the Christian world to the rosary. The Confraternity became extremely popular. Records show some 500,000 members in 1479, only four years after official papal approval of the organization. The requirements for membership were minimal, recitation of Our Lady's Psalter once per week and the reception of Holy Communion on the first Sunday of each month. The Confraternity generated or was the inspiration for many rosary books during the sixteenth century. These books were very influential in defining the fifteen mysteries as we have them today. The most successful of these rosary picture books was *Rosario Della Gloriosa Vergine* by the Dominican friar Alberto da Castello.

The second half of the sixteenth century saw the Confraternity's work rewarded, with the rosary's official recognition by the Church. The naval victory of Don Juan over the Turks at Lepanto (attributed to the rosary) on October 7, 1571 was the impetus needed to make Pope St. Pius V declare that henceforth a commemoration in honor of the rosary would be held on that day. Two years later, in 1573, Pope Gregory XIII established the Feast of the Most Holy Rosary; the feast still stands in the liturgical calendar.

Through the work of St. Louis de Montfort and his book *The Secret of the Rosary* the rosary became fixed in its contemporary format. In his book St. Louis was effectively able to integrate a history of the prayer with its practical application and recitation. Although the book was written in the late seventeenth century the rosary format used is the same as we have today. The importance of this book in finalizing the rosary format and eliminating the many versions which previously existed attests to its significance in the historical derivation of the rosary.

Chapter 3 — Notes

1. Many different versions of coronas or chaplets (as opposed to the standard term of rosary used today) grew up from use in different geographic locations and in the specific needs of religious communities. Examples of such prayer counters are the Brigettine corona, the chaplet of the Seven Dolors and the Schrocken corona.

2. In the British Museum, London, and the Smithsonian Institute, Washington, D.C., there are examples of late medieval and early Renaissance rosary artifacts that are arranged in the contemporary format of decades of smaller beads separated by larger beads. The precise use of the larger beads can only be hypothesized.

3. Herbert Thurston, S.J., "Our Popular Devotions II: The Rosary VII," *The Month* 97 (1901), p. 397.

4. Fourteenth century manuscripts from the archives of the Dominican Order in Cologne use the term "markieruugszeichen" or marker in reference to the larger beads or prayer counters (rosary).

5. Immanuel M. Casanowicz, "The Collection of Rosaries in the United States National Museum," *Proceedings of the United States National Museum*, no. 1667 (Washington, DC, 1909).

6. Franz Michel Willam, *The Rosary: Its History and Meaning*,

trans. Edwin Kaiser, C.P.P.S. (New York: Benziger Brothers, Inc., 1953), pp. 33-42.

7. Othmar Doerr, "The Our Father and Hail Mary in the Baumberg Hermit's Rule," *Das Institut der Inclusen in Suddeutschland* (Munster: Dom-Verlag, 1934), p. 53.

8. Marijan Zadnikar and Adam Wiehand, *Die Kartauser* (Cologne: Wienand Verlag, 1983), pp. 21-26.

9. Willam, *The Rosary*, p. 36.

10. Herbert Thurston, S.J., "Our Popular Devotions II: The Rosary; The Rosary Amongst the Carthusians," *The Month* 96 (1900), p. 521.

11. Maisie Ward, *The Splendor of the Rosary* (New York: Sheed and Ward, 1945), p. 46.

12. Herbert Thurston, S.J., "The History of the Rosary in All Countries," *Journal of the Society of Arts* (February 1902), p. 62.

13. The Brigettine corona with sixty-three Hail Marys, one for each year of the supposed life of Mary on earth, was made popular after St. Bridget's death. During the fifteenth through seventeenth centuries her revelations were highly esteemed and are the source of this particular corona.

14. J. G. Shaw, *The Story of the Rosary* (Milwaukee: The Bruce Publishing Company, 1954), p. 104.

15. *Ibid.*, pp. 104-5.

16. Among others, Capuchins, Franciscans and Vincentians have used coronas other than the normative five-decade rosary in their community prayer.

17. Eithne Wilkins, *The Rose-Garden Game* (London: Victor Gollancz, LTD, 1969), pp. 54-55. The specialized orders of religious knights formed during the Crusades such as the Teutonic Knights and the Knights of St. John saw the chaplet of beads as integral to their habits, as was the sword to their mission of protecting crusaders. Thus, such orders wore the beads with their swords.

18. See Revelation 12:1-6.

19. Analysis of fifteenth century paintings by Jan van Eyck and Andrea Mantegna show coronas other than the standard decade arrangement familiar today.

20. See Willam, *The Rosary*, especially pp. 40-42. Father Willam gives a detailed analysis of the derivation of the various forms of coronas and chaplets.

21. Ancient Roman tradition states that following the Ascension of Jesus, Mary stayed with the Apostles in Jerusalem until the time she departed with St. John for Ephesus to lead the Christian community there. Tradition claims that Mary lived sixty-three years, until the time of the Dormitian.

22. The scripturally based Seven Dolors of Mary created a natural arrangement for a chaplet of seven groups of seven beads. The three additional Hail Marys are early evidence for the idea of a rosary pendant. This devotion became popular in the seventeenth century with the Order of Servants of Mary (Servites) and devotion to Our Lady of Sorrows, celebrated now on September 15.

23. The Schrocken corona is a survivor of the evolutionary reality of the rosary. Its present arrangement is very interesting for its combination of clausulae, and the unusual number of *Aves* without *Paters*. Additionally, Irish influence is seen in maintaining only the biblical salutations to Mary (by Gabriel and Elizabeth) in the Hail Mary prayer. See Willam, *The Rosary*, pp. 61-62 for a complete description of this corona.

24. The reverse order of saying the pendant in the Schrocken corona is one additional oddity to this survivor of Renaissance piety.

25. As we have shown in chapters 2 and 3, the thirteenth century did not know of decades of *Aves* with introduction by *Paters*. Thus these two organizations promoted the Psalter as then practiced.

26. The position of Visitor represents the Dominican order in a particular country. He is the highest ranking Dominican official in the country.

27. Herbert Thurston, S.J., "Alan de Rupe and His Indulgence of 60,000 Years," *The Month* 100 (1902), pp. 298-99.

28. Shaw, *Rosary*, p. 84.

29. Sprenger was originally a disciple of de Rupe but decided to break with his mentor in order to push for papal approval of

the Rosary Confraternity. He felt modification to the original de Rupe concept, shedding the close association with the Dominican order, was needed to win Rome's approval.

30. The original registrars for Sprenger's Rosary Confraternity are kept in the Vatican archives.
31. Shaw, *Rosary*, p. 86.
32. Pope Sixtus IV in *Pastoris Acterni*, May 30, 1478, granted an indulgence of seven years if the weekly recitation of the rosary was done on Christmas, the Annunciation, Assumption or Nativity of Mary. See appendix for a summary of indulgences given to Confraternity members.
33. The genius of de Rupe's simple obligations was the catalyst to the rosary's promotion. As we will see, however, Sprenger's modification of adding more requirements did not adversely affect the spread of the prayer.
34. There can be no certainty on this question. Alanus left no other instructions in writing other than "Our Lady's Psalter be said once per week." If Alanus meant a full 150 *Aves* then the requirements laid down by Jacob Sprenger are not an addition but merely his interpretation of the original plan of Alanus de Rupe.
35. Early Confraternity manuals speak of a Psalter of five decades of *Aves* with a *Pater* and Glory Be used to introduce and conclude each decade. This form became known as the Dominican rosary and eventually became the standard for rosary devotion.
36. This can be found in the Rosary Confraternity book of Jacob Sprenger, 1476 (housed in the archives of the Cologne Dominicans, among other places).
37. Shaw, *Rosary*, p. 90.
38. *Ibid.*, p. 92.
39. Castello followed behind Alanus de Rupe and Jacob Sprenger in continuing promotion of the rosary and its confraternity. His book was enormously successful and was translated into French and German before the end of the century.
40. Willam, *The Rosary*, pp. 78-79.
41. *Salvatoris Domini*, encyclical letter of Pope St. Pius V, March

5, 1572, paragraph 3. See *The Rosary Papal Teachings*, trans. Rev. Paul J. Oligny, OFM (Boston: Daughters of St. Paul, 1980), p. 288.

42. Ibid., paragraph 6. See also appendix, no. 62.

43. "Norms Governing Liturgical Calendars," *Liturgy Documentary Series 6* (Washington, DC: USCC, 1984), p. 86, 139.

44. *The Roman Missal*, Eng. trans. of the *Sacramentary*, approved by the NCCB and confirmed by the Holy See (New York: Catholic Publishing Company, 1974), p. 717.

45. *Ibid.*

46. *Ibid.*

47. *The English-Latin Sacramentary for the United States of America* (New York: Benziger Brothers, 1966), p. 1925.

48. *Ibid.*, p. 1935.

49. *Ibid.*

50. *Ibid.*

51. As has been outlined in this chapter, the Dominican rosary became the standard upon which rosary devotion was practiced from the early seventeenth century forward. The Dominican Rosary Confraternity book of 1680 followed the five decade pattern of *Aves* with a *Pater* and a Glory Be introducing and concluding each decade.

52. St. Louis de Montfort, *The Secret of the Rosary*, trans. Mary Barbour, T.O.P. (Bayshore, NY: Montfort Fathers, 1976), p. 18. De Montfort states: "It [the rosary] was given to the Church by Saint Dominic who had received it from the Blessed Virgin as a powerful means of converting the Albigensians and other sinners."

53. Shaw, *Rosary*, p. 113.

54. De Montfort, *Secret of the Rosary*, p. 17.

55. *Ibid.*, p. 63.

56. St. Louis mentions all the great men and women of the sixteenth and seventeenth centuries. Whether these people were as instrumentally involved in rosary devotion as de Montfort suggests is a question for further research.

57. *The Secret of the Rosary* is prefaced by four introductions titled (1) A White Rose, (2) A Red Rose, (3) A Mystical Rose Tree and (4) A Rosebud.

58. De Montfort, *Secret of the Rosary*, p. 10.
59. *Ibid.*, p. 11.
60. *Ibid.*, p. 13.
61. *Ibid.*, p. 15.
62. *Ibid.*, p. 16.
63. De Montfort quotes from *De Dignitate Psalterii* by Blessed Alanus de Rupe among many others of the period.
64. De Montfort, *Secret of the Rosary*, p. 65.

Chapter 4
Pope Leo XIII —
Rosary Advocate and Defender

After the sixteenth century definition of the rosary and the work of St. Louis de Montfort in the seventeenth century, the rosary became an institution within the Roman Catholic Church. During this period all Catholics used the rosary beads for prayer; many people carried the beads on their person at all times. The post-Tridentine Church accepted many practices which, along with the era of calm following the turmoil of the Reformation, allowed the rosary to truly blossom as a usable prayer devotion for all the faithful.

Our story of the rosary continues in the latter nineteenth century with the pontificate of Leo XIII. During his twenty-five year reign as Pope, 1878 to 1903, coming in the aftermath of Vatican I, he tried to consolidate a Church which was being pressured by the liberal policies of government and society into accepting a lesser role in world influence. The effects of the French Revolution were still very much in evidence throughout Europe. Because of this situation, Vatican I answered the tide of secularism in popular opinion by defining the concept of papal infallibility. Through this tense time period came Giocchino Vincenzo Pecci, who took the name of Leo XIII when he was installed as Pope in 1878. As a means to settle the unrest which the Church was suffering, Leo turned to the rosary as a means of devotion to again bring unity to the Church. During his reign on the chair of Peter, Leo published twelve encyclicals on the rosary and its devotion. Each of these letters, published almost annually in September or October, reinforced the efficacious nature of the rosary and its importance in our daily lives.

There is no question that Pope Leo XIII's influence on the rosary and its devotion was the most significant ever to come from the papal office. Much of what Leo said led to the greatest popularity which the rosary enjoyed during the high period of popular devotion in the first half of the twentieth century. Moreover, the pope's statements were the basis for additional twentieth century teachings in various documents, including later papal proclamations.

Pope Leo XIII's Writings

The first major work which Leo wrote on the theme of the rosary was *Supremi apostolatus*, which was published September 1, 1883. In this letter Leo reviews some of the history that led to the rosary devotion which then existed. Quoting his predecessors Urban IV, Sixtus IV and Gregory XIII, Leo expressed gratitude for the tributes of these men and others to the furthering of the rosary devotion.[1] A historical overview of the events in Christian history which contributed to rosary devotion is also mentioned. Although, as we have noted, the facts do not support the belief, Leo speaks of St. Dominic's rooting out of the Albigensian heresy through the rosary. The Battle of Lepanto and the subsequent definition of Pope St. Pius V is also mentioned in the letter.[2]

The most significant contribution of *Supremi Apostolatus* to the overall theology of the rosary was the institution of October as the month of special devotion to the rosary. As the annual memorial of Lepanto drew near Leo wrote, "Now that the anniversary of manifold and exceedingly great favors obtained by a

Christian people through the devotion of the rosary is at hand, we desire that the same devotion should be offered by the whole Catholic world with the greatest earnestness to the Blessed Virgin, in order that by her intercession the Lord's hand may be appeased and moved to compassion toward us in the miseries which afflict us."[3] Leo points out that it has been the practice of Catholics for centuries to fly to Mary for refuge during times of danger and strife. Therefore, he exhorts the faithful, "Not only do we earnestly exhort all Christians to give themselves to the pious recital of the rosary publicly, or privately in their own home and family, and so unceasingly, but we also desire that the whole of the month of October be consecrated to the Holy Queen of the Rosary."[4] Thus, the month of October became the one special month celebrated annually in recognition of the merits of the rosary.

Later in 1883, Pope Leo gave more amplification to his September encyclical. In the apostolic letter *Salutaris ille*, published on December 24, 1883, Leo states that each Christian family should not allow a day to pass without reciting the rosary: "We exhort and beseech all the faithful to persevere religiously and faithfully in the daily use of the rosary; and we declare it to be our wish that it be recited every day in the principal church of each diocese and on feast days in all parish churches."[5]

Superiore anno, published August 30, 1884, was Leo's second encyclical written on the subject of the rosary. The major theme of this work is the preservation of the custom of rosary prayer and its devotion. He states, "Care must be taken, therefore, to preserve the holy custom of reciting the rosary of Mary, particularly because this method of prayer is arranged to recall all the mysteries of our salvation, and so is eminently fitted to foster the spirit of piety."[6] Through the prayerful use of the rosary the faithful can gain the grateful assistance and support of Mary. This important idea should not be overlooked as trite or useless. On the contrary, Leo states: "we have deemed it our duty again this year to exhort the people of Christendom to persevere in that method and formula of prayer known as the rosary of Mary, and thereby to merit the powerful patronage of the great Mother of God."[7]

Leo never seemed to leave out the rosary and its devotion in whatever he wrote. An example of such an opportunity is found in his encyclical *Quod auctoritate* of December 22, 1885. Here, while proclaiming an extraordinary jubilee, the pope continues to stress the importance of rosary devotion. He stated, "And if we stress this exhortation, as we have already done several times, not one of you will be surprised, for you understand how important it is that the custom of Mary's rosary should flourish among Christians. You are also well aware that it is a part and a very beautiful form of that spirit of prayer which we speak of, that it is made for our times, is easy to practice and fruitful in results."[8]

From our earlier discussion we remember that the Feast of the Most Holy Rosary became a universal celebration during the pontificate of Clement XI in 1716. In his letter *Vi e ben noto* to the bishops of Italy, written September 20, 1887, Pope Leo elevated the nature of the feast: "We decree that the Solemnity of the Holy Rosary be raised to the rite of 'Double of the Second Class' for the whole Church."[9] This level would correlate closely with the term "memorial" as defined by the revised General Norms for the Liturgical Year and Calendar published in 1969; the feast is currently celebrated in such a manner. In this letter, as in all previous writings, Pope Leo speaks of the importance of maintaining devotion to the rosary. He stated, "We are equally persuaded that devotion to the Virgin (under the title of Queen of the Rosary) brings help in the very special needs of our times. Therefore, we wish this devotion to be everywhere revived and to be more firmly established among the faithful all over the world."[10]

In September of 1891 Pope Leo wrote some of his most significant words about the rosary. Published September 22, Leo's encyclical letter *Octobri mense* emphasizes prayer through the mediation of Mary with special significance given to the mysteries of the rosary. Leo states, "With equal truth it may be said that of the great treasury of all graces given to us by Our Lord — (for grace and truth came by Jesus Christ) — nothing comes to us except through the mediation of Mary, for such is the will of God."[11] For Leo, as would seem quite evident, the principal way to reach God through Mary is through the rosary. Leo expresses this quite beautifully: "For this reason we especially mention by name and recommend the rosary. Common language has given the name 'crown' to this manner of prayer, which recalls to our minds the great mysteries of Jesus and Mary united in joys, sorrows and triumphs. The contemplation of these august mysteries, considered in their due order, gives to faithful souls a wonderful strengthening of faith, protects them against error, and fortifies their souls."[12]

It seems that the writings of Pope Leo had great positive effect in bringing the rosary to many peoples. Additionally, the rosary was gaining popularity and became a source of inspiration to many. In response to the great outpouring on behalf of the Catholic faithful, Leo wrote in *Octobri mense*, "the rosary . . . has always been highly cherished and widely used in private and in public, in homes, and in families, in the meetings of confraternities, at the dedication of shrines and in solemn processions."[13] Evidently Leo's passion for Mary and the rosary had become contagious and spread throughout the world.

In September 1892, Leo wrote one of his most famous rosary encyclicals, *Magnae Dei Matris*. In this letter, the pope stressed the importance of the rosary as the most appropriate form of prayer to Mary. Prayer itself is the most important overall idea in the letter. The document rings with the feeling of one who deeply believes in the efficacy of prayer and of the great need to seek Mary as the great intercessor for all Christians. Leo wrote, "It is therefore a fitting and opportune time to prepare to celebrate the coming month of October, consecrated to Our Lady as the august Queen of the Rosary, with the fervent and wholehearted devotion which the necessities weighing upon us demand."[14]

For the first time in his pontificate, Leo in *Magnae Dei Matris* speaks of the rosary as a devotion which can unlock the chief mysteries of the Christian faith. He states, "We may add that the Rosary offers an easy way to penetrate the chief mysteries of the Christian religion and to impress them upon the mind."[15] Through prayerful recitation of the rosary, the Paschal mystery, the life, death and resurrection of Jesus, can be unlocked and become part of our daily life. Making the central mystery of our faith part of our daily life can do nothing other than draw us closer to God and our common Christian vocation to holiness. In unlocking the chief mysteries of the Faith, the rosary has in many ways been a tool of education. Leo recognized this as well: "To ward off the exceedingly great dangers of ignorance from her children, the Church . . . has been in the habit of looking for the staunchest support of faith in the rosary of Mary."[16]

Magnae Dei Matris speaks of the spirit of prayer and its efficacious fulfillment in devotion to the rosary. The rosary is very much a prayer of the whole Church. Consequently, the Church, the faith community, must use this prayer to achieve its powerful help. Leo points out that Mary was given the unique prerogative above all other women to be Mother of Jesus. The mercy she shows to us is a true gift; we must go to Mary using her help to reach her son.

Written on the occasion of the fiftieth anniversary of his episcopal ordination, *Laetitae sanctae*, published September 8, 1893, speaks in more general terms of the healing power of the rosary and its benefits for both individuals and society at large. The healing powers of the rosary are described principally through a discussion of the joyful, sorrowful and glorious mysteries.[17] Prayerful devotion to the rosary and its fifteen mysteries can help cure the ills of individuals leading to healing of all society. Leo stated, "For evils such as these let us seek a remedy in the rosary, which consists in a fixed order of prayer combined with devout meditation on the life of Christ and his Blessed Mother. . . . For we are convinced that the rosary, if devoutly used, is bound to benefit not only the individual, but society at large."[18]

The idea that the rosary could be a benefit to both individuals and society was a rather unique idea for the time. Although the Rosary Confraternity of Blessed Alanus de Rupe was based on a group of people who all prayed the rosary, such practice had been neglected since the time of St. Louis de Montfort. There really was no concept of common recitation in the nineteenth century, nor any thought that the benefits received from prayer could be felt throughout the community. Pope Leo's insight was important, therefore, in showing how the rosary was a prayer for the whole Church, not just individuals. He wrote, "Who, then, can fail to see how great and rich is the saving power of Mary's holy rosary and what admirable remedies present-day society can draw from it to heal its ills and prevent their return?"[19]

As September 1894 rolled round Pope Leo was again writing about the rosary and its importance for Catholic Christians. In *Iucunda semper* the pope wrote of maintaining the importance of the rosary while continuing to exhort the faithful to the efficacious intercessory power of Mary. Apparently Leo felt that devotion to the rosary was not sufficiently honored within the faith community. To bring more attention to this subject Leo made this an important theme of his encyclical. He wrote, "It is our ardent wish that this devotion [to the rosary] shall be restored to a place of honor in the city and in the village, in the family and in the workshop, in the noble's house and in the peasants', that it be to all a dear devotion and a noble sign of their faith, that it be a sure way to the gaining of the favor of pardon."[20]

The concept of hope comes through clearly in the Pope's desire to further the understanding of Mary's intercessory powers. Leo contends that aid should be sought through the intercession of Mary and through the express means of the rosary, "which Christians have ever found to be of marvelous value."[21] By turning to Mary, our hope for the world should significantly increase. This hope is manifested specifically in Mary's Psalter. Leo wrote, "We place our best hope in the holy rosary inasmuch as more than any other means it can implore from God the help that we need."[22] It seems that for Leo the more fixed one's thought is upon the rosary, the clearer the hope and power of this devotion becomes.

For Pope Leo XIII there was not a purpose or occasion within the Church where the rosary could not be an effective way of reaching God through Mary. As pointed out in *Laetitae sanctae* the rosary can heal the wounds of society as well as personal problems. Realizing this, Pope Leo entered a sensitive area in *Adiutricem populi*. Published September 5, 1895, this encyclical letter dealt with the topic of ecumenism. Although the practical application of what Leo said is very slight, the fact remains that to him the rosary could be used as the perfect prayer for unity in the reality of divided Christendom.[23]

Leo put forth some very practical ideas on how the rosary could be used to further Christian unity. For Leo the rosary was the best tool to nurture faith. By meditation upon its mysteries, the rosary dispelled ignorance and reduced the danger of error. Of course, Leo's idea was that all Christian faiths separated from Catholicism should return to the fold. Leo wrote, "We say that the rosary is by far the best prayer by which to plead before her the cause of our separated brethren."[24] Even though this is inconsistent with contemporary ecumenical thought, the concept that the rosary could be effective in returning Christianity to one united fold was both novel and insightful. Leo was ahead of his time in seeking a solution to one of the biggest problems in Christianity today.

In *Adiutricem populi* Pope Leo again states his ever-present theme that the rosary is the most efficacious of prayer forms to our Blessed Mother. He states, "it gives us the greatest pleasure to recall, that of all the forms of devotion to the Blessed Virgin, that most excellent method of prayer, Mary's Rosary, is establishing itself most widely in popular esteem and practice."[25] Additionally, the encyclical states, "There are, of course, more ways than one to win her protection by prayer but, as for us, we think that the best and most effective way to her lies in her rosary."[26] Seeing Mary as the bond between humanity and God is important in Pope Leo's thought. He states, "Mary will be the happy bond to draw together with strong yet gentle constraint all who love Christ."[27] Certainly for Leo this bond is best achieved through efficacious devotion to Mary's rosary.

Pope Leo continued his 1890s series of encyclical letters on the rosary with the publication September 20, 1896 of *Fidentem piumque*, A Perfect Prayer. In the letter, Leo highlights themes that have been present in some of his earlier writings. He calls for daily recitation of the rosary in the cathedral church of each diocese and writes that the rosary should be recited every feast day in parish churches.[28] Such practice will further the communal recitation of the rosary on the world scale. In this encyclical also, Pope Leo, as in *Magnae Dei Matris*, emphasizes the importance of the rosary for its unlocking of the principal mysteries of the faith. He wrote, "So may the sublime mysteries of this same faith be more deeply impressed in men's minds by means of the rosary devotion, with the happy result that 'we may imitate what they contain and obtain what they promise.'"[29]

As the long pontificate of Pope Leo XIII reached its height in the late 1890s, the words of praise of Mary continued to flow from his pen. In the publication of *Augustissimae Virginis* September 12, 1897, the pope continued to outline the importance of devotion to Mary, especially through her rosary. He wrote, "Whoever considers the height of dignity to which God has raised the most august Virgin Mary will easily perceive how important it is, both for the public and private good, that devotion to her should be assiduously practiced and daily promoted more and more."[30] By turning to Mary and her rosary Leo was convinced that the lagging piety of the faithful would be strengthened. The pope wrote, "We would not willingly leave you without our letter this year, once more urging you with all possible earnestness to strive by the recitation of the rosary to aid both yourselves individually and the universal Church in her needs."[31]

In *Augustissimae Virginis*, Leo speaks of the importance of the Confraternity of the Rosary. The pope summarizes the traditional Dominican influence on the rosary and its origin. He then states, "But the power and efficacy of the rosary appear all the greater when we consider it as a duty imposed on the Confraternity which bears its name."[32] At the time of the pope's writing the popularity of the Rosary Confraternity had waned a bit. It was Leo's hope that by his exhortation the Confraternity would once again become an important organization to aid the faithful in their spiritual journey.

During the twentieth year of his reign upon the chair of Peter, Pope Leo wrote his last encyclical letter on the subject of the rosary. Published September 5, 1898, *Diuturni temporis* was the pope's last effort to bring the rosary to all the faithful. As in the past, his theme did not waver much: the way to Mary was through her rosary. The pope wrote, "The Marian rosary, in fact, is a wonderful garland woven of the Angelic salutation, interspersed with the Lord's Prayer, combined with the obligation of meditation. It is a most excellent manner of praying . . . and very fruitful for the attainment of eternal life."[33]

Pope Leo's idea of reaffirming the Confraternity of the Rosary came to full fruition in the apostolic constitution *Ubi primum*, published October 2, 1898. The Confraternity, described in *Diuturni temporis*, is given sixteen bolstering articles in *Ubi primum* outlining the structure, organization, purpose and works of the Rosary Confraternity.[34] Pope Leo gives the Dominican order and its master general the task of overseeing the Confraternity and its works.[35] With the reestablished influence of the Confraternity in place, Pope Leo had completed his great work of bringing the rosary to a position of prominence within the prayer and devotional life of the faithful.

Summary

The work of Pope Leo XIII in promotion of the rosary is a landmark in the evolving history of this most glorious prayer of devotion to Mary. More than any other pontiff, Leo wrote extensively on the rosary, completing twelve encyclicals and numerous other letters, apostolic exhortations and similar works. In his twenty-five year pontificate Leo touched on all aspects of the rosary devotion. All of his teachings, however, were centered about the concept that by using the rosary one could most efficaciously reach Mary, and through her intercession, her son Jesus Christ.

Pope Leo's early encyclicals emphasized the importance of devotion to Mary and how this could best be accomplished through use of the rosary. Leo wanted to restore the rosary to a prominent position within the devotional life of the Church. His work was most certainly successful, as evidenced by the great popularity of the rosary during the first half of the twentieth century. Additionally, during the early period of Leo's pontificate he wrote encyclicals which emphasized the mysteries of the rosary and Mary as the principal mediatrix.

Beginning with the publication of *Magnae Dei Matris* in September 1892, Leo's message began to take a more wide-ranging perspective. Through the encyclical *Fidentem piumque* the Pope outlined how the rosary could be used to unlock the chief mysteries of the Christian faith. In *Laetitae sanctae* the pope spoke of the benefits of the rosary. These benefits were given both individually and communally; the rosary became a means to heal the ills of society. In *Adiutricem populi* the pope spoke of the importance of the rosary as a means to help achieve unity within Christendom. Although by today's standards this overture toward ecumenism was slight, the significance of such a move in the 1890s is noteworthy. Finally through the reestablishment of the Confraternity of the Rosary (*Diuturni temporis* and *Ubi primum*) under the supervision of the Dominican order, the rosary was ready to take its rightful place as a powerful means of devotion to Mary and praise of God.

The work of Pope Leo XIII was noteworthy too in making the rosary an important devotional prayer at the dawn of our century. As we will see, the twentieth century has provided a rich history for the development of this most efficacious of intercessory prayers.

Chapter 4 — Notes

1. *Supremi Apostolatus*, encyclical letter of Pope Leo XIII, September 1, 1883, paragraph 16. This document and all the encyclicals of Pope Leo XIII are found in *The Papal Encyclopedia*, vol. 2, ed. Claudia Ihm (Raleigh, NC: McGrath Publishing Company, 1981).
2. *Ibid.*, paragraphs 13 and 14.
3. *Ibid.*, paragraph 2.
4. *Ibid.*, paragraph 22.
5. *Salutaris ille*, apostolic letter of Pope Leo XIII, December 24, 1883, paragraph 6. See *Papal Teachings; The Holy Rosary*, trans. Rev. Paul J. Oligny, OFM (Boston: Daughters of St. Paul, 1980), p. 56.
6. *Superiore anno*, encyclical letter of Pope Leo XIII, August 30, 1884, paragraph 5.
7. *Ibid.*, paragraph 4.
8. *Quod auctoritate*, encyclical letter of Pope Leo XIII, December 22, 1885, paragraph 2.
9. *Vi e ben noto*, letter of Pope Leo XIII to the bishops of Italy, September 20, 1887, paragraph 4. See *Papal Teachings; The Holy Rosary*, p. 62.
10. *Ibid.*, paragraph 1.
11. *Octobri mense*, encyclical letter of Pope Leo XIII, September 22, 1891, paragraph 11.

12. *Ibid.*, paragraph 15.
13. *Ibid.*, paragraph 14.
14. *Magnae Dei Matris*, encyclical letter of Pope Leo XIII, September 7, 1892.
15. *Ibid.*, paragraph 13.
16. *Ibid.*, paragraph 17.
17. *Laetitae sanctae*, encyclical letter of Pope Leo XIII, September 8, 1893, paragraphs 13-15, 24-29.
18. *Ibid.*, paragraph 4.
19. *Ibid.*, paragraph 28.
20. *Iucunda semper*, encyclical letter of Pope Leo XIII, September 8, 1894.
21. *Ibid.*, paragraph 1.
22. *Ibid.*, paragraph 20.
23. During the period of Leo XIII's reign ecumenism was a very restricted and limited topic. Catholicism had not enjoyed the *aggiornamento* of Vatican II. Thus, the pope's overtures to other Christians was praiseworthy. The rosary seemed the ideal prayer for such an effort.
24. *Adiutricem populi*, encyclical letter of Pope Leo XIII, September 5, 1895, paragraph 27.
25. *Ibid.*, paragraph 2.
26. *Ibid.*, paragraph 23.
27. *Ibid.*, paragraph 17.
28. *Fidentem piumque*, encyclical letter of Pope Leo XIII, September 20, 1896, paragraph 6.
29. *Ibid.*, paragraph 22.
30. *Augustissimae Virginis*, encyclical letter of Pope Leo XIII, September 12, 1897.
31. *Ibid.*, paragraph 6.
32. *Ibid.*, paragraph 17.
33. *Diuturni temporis*, encyclical letter of Pope Leo September 5, 1898, paragraph 5.
34. *Ubi primum*, apostolic constitution of Pope Leo XIII, October 2, 1898, paragraph 3ff.
35. *Ibid.*, paragraphs 4 and 5.

Chapter 5
The Rosary in the
Twentieth Century

The story that we have heretofore outlined about the rosary does not end with the pontificate of Leo XIII. Significant teachings about the rosary continued to come forth both from Rome and other prominent sources within the Church. Following the reign of Leo XIII, the rosary enjoyed its most popular period in the first half of our century. Together with novenas, parish missions and other forms of popular devotion, the rosary truly became the prayer for all people. Its popularity and use during this period of history was never greater.

At the dawn of the twentieth century the rosary we know today was basically set in place. The recitation of five decades together with the mysteries of the day (joyful on Mondays and Thursdays, sorrowful on Tuesdays and Fridays and glorious on Wednesdays, Saturdays and Sundays), preceded by the pendant of the Apostles' Creed, Our Father, three Hail Marys and doxology was the normative prayer of rosary devotion. The recitation of all fifteen decades still was conducted but rarely in public. As has been noted previously, some religious communities continued to use a special pattern of beads and prayers under the term rosary. For most people, however, the earlier work of St. Louis de Montfort had set the trend for rosary recitation and devotion.

As the twentieth century began to unfold rosary devotion began to develop in various ways. Without question the most significant event which promoted rosary devotion during this period was the apparitions of Mary at Fatima, a small village in central Portugal. In her appearances to the three young children Mary's message was clear — pray the rosary for peace and the reparation of sins (Fatima is the subject of chapter 8 of this book). As a result of Fatima, promotion of the rosary was greatly furthered on all fronts. Documents from Rome continued to pour forth espousing the merits of this most important devotion.[1] Additionally, personal and communal recitation of the rosary became more pronounced as the faithful responded to Mary's message of hope and peace.

The Church Speaks

The Church continued to speak out in official proclamations throughout the first half of the twentieth century. One interesting phenomenon which continued to follow rosary devotion was the apocryphal account of the prayer's origination with St. Dominic. In the letter *In Coetu soladium* (October 29, 1916) Pope Benedict XV stated, "The Church has most certainly received from the hands of Dominic and of his disciples that powerful help against heretics and vices which is found in the Marian rosary."[2] In an even more dramatic way, Pope Pius XI in his letter *Inclytam ac Perillustrem* (March 6, 1934) credited the Virgin Mary herself with giving St. Dominic the rosary. He stated, "Among the weapons St. Dominic used to convert the heretics the most efficacious, as the faithful well know, was the Marian rosary, the practice of which, taught by the Blessed Virgin herself, has so widely spread throughout the Catholic world."[3]

Although confusion about the rosary's origin continued to be a major factor in papal teachings, the more important idea of the value of the rosary in daily prayer and reflection was predominant.

Pope Benedict XV exhorted the faithful to pray the rosary. In a letter to Father Becchi of the Dominican order the pope asks the people to pray the rosary every day, as "it is the most beautiful flower of human piety and the most fruitful font of heavenly graces."[4] Pope Pius XI in his letter *Inclytam ac Perillustrem* expressed a similar note: "We ardently desire that the custom of the daily recitation of the rosary in alternate praise, considered so sacred for the Christian family, be religiously preserved or restored."[5]

During the pontificates of popes Pius XI and Pius XII the concept of communal celebration of the rosary became popular. The influence of Fatima is significant in this transformation to common recitation.[6] Additionally, both of the popes wrote in support of such a devotion. In the encyclical *Ingravescentibus malis* (September 29, 1937), Pius XI wrote, "Among the public prayers which we profitably address to the Virgin Mother of God, the holy rosary occupies a special and exceptional place."[7] The Pope admonished those people who would discount the efficacy of the prayer saying that the rosary was intended for all peoples at all times. In the same letter, Pius states that communal celebration of the rosary is profitable for the whole Catholic community. He wrote, "Above all it [the rosary] nourishes the Catholic Faith which by timely meditation on the sacred mysteries gains new strength, and it lifts the mind to the contemplation of divinely revealed truths."[8]

Pope Pius XII in his encyclical letter *Ingruentium malorum* (September 19, 1951) concentrates on confidence in the rosary's efficacy, especially when celebrated within a family setting. For the pope, confidence was built in knowing that the rosary had always helped people when adversity struck. He wrote, "We do not hesitate to affirm again publicly that we put great confidence in the holy rosary for the healing of evils that afflict our times."[9] Certainly for Pope Pius XII, the rosary itself was an efficacious tool in our journey to God. Yet, the more basic idea underlying his thought was the importance of Mary and her role in aiding men and women to attain salvation. Again in *Ingruentium malorum* Pius XII wrote so beautifully, "Always turn with ever increasing confidence to the Virgin Mother of God to whom Christians have always and principally resorted, in as much as she was constituted the source of salvation for the whole human race."[10]

The one certain way to assure the full benefit of the rosary was by its use within a Christian family. This became almost a battle cry of the 1950s. Pope Pius XII also was an advocate of family devotion to the special prayers of Mary. This idea was noted well when he wrote, "But it is above all within families that we desire that the custom of the holy rosary should everywhere flourish again, be religiously preserved and constantly fostered."[11] Pope Pius continued his campaign to show the importance of the family rosary. In a letter to the assistant director of the Apostleship of Prayer the Pope wrote, "They [those in the Apostleship of Prayer] should recite the rosary everyday, as often as possible with the entire family gathered at home."[12] In July 1952 the Pope was even more overt when he wrote in a letter to Cardinal Griffin, "What form of collective prayer could be more simple and yet more efficacious than the family rosary. . . . There is no surer means of calling down God's blessings upon the family and especially of preserving peace and happiness in the home than the daily recitation of the rosary." The insight of Pope Pius XII fits in well with another man whose name today is synonymous with rosary devotion.

The Rosary Priest — Patrick Peyton, C.S.C.

During this century no person's name has had more association with the rosary than Father Patrick Peyton. As the rallying cry for family recitation of the rosary began, Father Peyton, a Holy Cross priest, made it a common family practice within the Roman Catholic community. Father Peyton's expression, "The family that prays together, stays together"[14] became his trademark in a career of rosary crusades that would take him all over the world in his message to pray the rosary.

Patrick Peyton was born in Carracastle, county Mayo, Ireland on January 9, 1909, the sixth of nine children. Life at that time in

Ireland was difficult but through perseverance and hard work the family managed to survive on their country farm. It was in these early years that Patrick Peyton became convinced of the importance of family prayer. His father, John, would gather the family for prayer and lead them in the recitation of the rosary mysteries. From the good example of his father, Patrick continued this practice in his later life as a religious priest and rosary crusader.

The events that would launch the future career of Patrick began at the University of Notre Dame in South Bend, Indiana. Patrick and his older brother Tom had arrived in the United States in May 1928 to pursue an education. Befriended by a priest from Scranton, Pennsylvania, Monsignor Paul Kelly, Patrick and Tom eventually wound up at Notre Dame enrolled in the minor seminary program for the Congregation of Holy Cross.[15] After finishing high school and college at Notre Dame, Patrick moved to Washington, D.C. to begin his graduate theology studies.

In February 1939 Patrick's life took an abrupt turn when he was diagnosed as having tuberculosis. After three months in a local hospital Patrick was returned to the infirmary at Notre Dame for treatment. When the doctors in September 1939 declared that treatment had been a failure Patrick resorted to his last hope, total trust in God through invocation of Mary the Mother of Jesus. On Halloween day 1939 Patrick's prayers were answered. Peyton states in his autobiography, "Just then the oppression and depression and the darkness were swept from my soul, to be replaced by a lightness, a freedom and a hope."[16] Within two weeks the excessive fluid levels in Patrick's lungs were almost gone. On January 15, 1940, the doctors at Heathwin Sanitarium in South Bend, Indiana declared Patrick cured and recommended his return to theological study. Through prayers to the Virgin Mary Patrick Peyton had been cured; he would never forget his reprieve from death in dedicating his life to furthering rosary devotion.

In January 1942, following his ordination, Patrick discovered how he would spend his life in thanking Mary for her many gifts to him. Realizing a world at war in Europe and remembering the efficacy of the rosary at Lepanto in 1571, Patrick began to chart his future course. As he stated: "That was the decision I made, to devote my entire life, my every effort, to the promotion of family prayer and particularly of family prayer expressed in the form of the rosary said every day or night by the family gathered together in its own home."[17]

In the latter part of 1942 Father Peyton began his program of family prayer and rosary devotion. He initially received the permission and support of his religious superiors in Holy Cross and the American Catholic Bishops (through the influence of Bishop, later Cardinal John Francis O'Hara of Philadelphia)[18] to begin a campaign to further family prayer and rosary devotion. By February 1947, Father Peyton, by enlisting the support of many movie and theater personalities, was able to initiate radio programs under the banner of the "Family Theater of the Air." These programs, broadcast by the mutual radio network, were nonsectarian shows designed to further the family as the basic unit of contemporary civilization. The founding of Family Theater prefigured the future course of Father Peyton's ministry.

The future for Father Peyton's rosary crusade was bright. In the late 1940s Father Peyton began a series of rosary crusades which would take him to all parts of the world many times over. Held generally in large outdoor plazas and stadiums, these crusades drew millions of people. The message was always the same — pray the rosary and pray it as a family. Over the years Father Peyton's contacts greatly increased until he came to be recognized internationally as "The Rosary Priest."[19] Through the encouragement of friends and supporters, together with many contributors, Family Theater, headquartered in Hollywood, California, was able to produce many shows for radio, television and film. The response to these programs has been overwhelming over the years. Even the late Princess Grace of Monaco assisted Father Peyton in his film presentations of the fifteen mysteries.[20]

The influence of Father Patrick Peyton on rosary devotion in the twentieth century cannot be overestimated. Today he continues to work ever diligently to further the rosary and family prayer. Through this work the name of Patrick Peyton has become synonymous with rosary devotion. Although contemporary rosary devotion has moved into what Father Peyton calls "an eclipse," he believes that as the sun returns to shine brightly when the eclipse finishes, so will the rosary return to its proper place of devotion.[21]

Recent Developments

There is no question that the last twenty to thirty years have seen a decrease in rosary devotion throughout the Catholic world. Part of the reason for this situation lies in the fact that all popular devotion has been usurped by a return to a more fundamental and basic understanding of the eucharistic liturgy. No one can argue that the Mass is the most central prayer worship within the Catholic Church. Consequently the Second Vatican Council reemphasized the eucharistic liturgical celebration, especially with the use of the vernacular language in its celebration. The faithful became better able to understand the Mass, and therefore became greater participants in its celebration.

Despite the reduction in universal rosary devotion, this most beautiful of Marian devotions continued to captivate the imaginations of popes and other Church officials through their writings and official Church proclamations. In his encyclical letter *Grata recordatio*, Pope John XXIII spoke in loving remembrance of Pope Leo XIII and all he had done to promote rosary devotion. By remembering the work of Pope Leo XIII one could trustfully pray to God through Mary's intercession for favors needed. In the letter, Pope John exhorted the faithful to recite the rosary each day, "with special devotion."[22] Summing up the efficacious nature of the rosary the pope wrote, "The rosary, as is known to all, is, in fact, a very excellent means of prayer and meditation in the form of a mystical crown in which the prayers Our Father, Hail Mary and Glory Be to the Father are intertwined with meditation on the greatest mysteries of our faith and which presents to the mind, like many pictures, the drama of the Incarnation of Our Lord and the Redemption [of humankind]."[23]

Besides repeating what previous pontiffs had said about the

rosary, Pope John expanded the teachings in new directions. In *Oecumenicum Concilium* (April 28, 1962) the pope speaks of the rosary as "A prayer of love breathed from the heart."[24] From the outset of his reign, Pope John spoke of the rosary as a form of prayer and meditation. In *Grata recordatio* (September 26, 1959) the idea of meditation is first introduced.[25] In his apostolic letter *Il religioso convegnor* (September 29, 1961), however, Pope John's teaching took a great leap forward. In this letter he outlined the three-fold meditative intentions for the rosary: mystical contemplation, intimate reflection and pious intention. The Pope wrote, "The true substance of the well-meditated rosary consists in a three-fold element that gives unity and cohesion to the social expression, unfolding in vivid succession the episodes which join together the life of Jesus and Mary, in reference to the different conditions of the persons praying and to the aspirations of the universal Church. For each decade of Hail Marys there is a picture, and for each picture a three-fold emphasis which is simultaneously: mystical contemplation, intimate reflection and pious intention."[26]

Pope Paul VI continued to show papal support for the rosary. The Pope emphasized the prayerful recitation of the rosary with the mysteries as the prime mode of meditation. In the apostolic exhortation *Marialis Cultus* (February 2, 1974), the pope wrote, "Without this [contemplation] the rosary is a body without a soul, and its recitation is in danger of becoming a mechanical repetition of formulas and of going counter to the warning of Christ."[27] Additionally, the pope stated concerning the mysteries of the rosary, "Meditation on the mysteries of the rosary by familiarizing the hearts and minds of the faithful with the mysteries of Christ, can be an excellent preparation for the celebration of those same mysteries in echo thereof."[28]

Other themes concerning the rosary and its importance come forth in the text of *Marialis Cultus*. First, Pope Paul wants to affirm with his predecessors the importance of family prayer. He states, "We now desire, as a continuation of the thought of our predecessors, to recommend strongly the recitation of the family rosary."[29] Another important theme in this letter is how clearly the rosary is a prayer which easily associates itself with the mystery of the Church's liturgical life. Pope Paul wrote, "As a Gospel prayer, centered on the mystery of the redemptive incarnation, the rosary is, therefore, a prayer with a clearly Christological orientation.[30] Again the pope wrote, "the rosary is a practice of piety which easily harmonizes with the liturgy."[31]

In his encyclical *Mense maio* (April 29, 1965), Pope Paul continued to expound on the importance of the rosary, especially as an encounter with Christ. He wrote: "do not fail to inculcate the practice of the Marian rosary. It is a form of prayer very dear to the Virgin Mother of God and so highly recommended by the Supreme Pontiffs."[32] Pope Paul emphasizes the fact that Mary is only a source, albeit a very important one, which leads to Christ. Thus through the rosary one comes in contact with Christ, especially through meditation upon the mysteries. In *Mense maio* Pope Paul wrote, "Mary remains ever the path that leads to Christ. Every encounter with her can only result in an encounter with Christ himself."[33]

In his encyclical *Christi Matri* (September 15, 1966), Pope Paul strongly recommended prayer and devotion to the Mother of God. The Pope wrote, "We can see nothing more appropriate or efficacious than the whole Christian family to raise its voice amid its many stresses and difficulties to the Mother of God, whom we address as Queen of Peace."[34] The pope goes on to make more specific his generic comments on devotion to Mary. As would be appropriate the rosary came to the forefront because of its efficacious nature and universal appeal. The pope wrote, "And for that reason we are anxious for you . . . to give a lead and urge by exhortation a more persevering prayer to the gracious Virgin Mary by the devout recitation of the rosary. . . . This prayer is well suited to God's people, acceptable to the Mother of God and powerful in obtaining gifts from heaven."[35]

During his pontificate Pope Paul wrote many letters to organizations and individuals who promoted rosary devotion. In an allocution to children of the living rosary written May 10, 1964, he states, "Through your rosary you can succeed in giving comfort to the sick, in saving the dying, in converting sinners, in helping the missionaries and in freeing the souls from purgatory."[36] As with his predecessors Pius XII and John XXIII, Pope Paul carried on a vigorous correspondence with the aforementioned Father Patrick Peyton. In a letter of March 12, 1964 addressed to Father Peyton, the Pope wrote, "We, therefore, warmly recommend the Family Rosary crusade, which inculcates the practice of daily prayer, of family prayer and of prayer by means of the rosary."[37]

Even the contemporary Church has continued the practice of promoting the rosary as a means to God, and therefore, as an asset along the road to salvation. In its pastoral letter "Behold Your Mother — Woman of Faith" of November 1973, the National Conference of Catholic Bishops warns against rejection of the rosary because of its ancient roots: "It is unwise to reject the rosary without a trial simply because of the accusation that it comes from the past, that it is repetitious and ill-suited to sophisticated moderns. The Scriptural riches of the rosary are of permanent value."[38] In this letter the bishops recommend that the traditional fifteen mysteries be expanded to incorporate more of the many incidents in the life of Christ upon which meditation would be fruitful. Such a means of expanding or substituting new mysteries can only lead to a greater understanding of discipleship.[39] In their 1983 pastoral letter "The Challenge of Peace," the American bishops summarized much of the historical value of the rosary when they stated, "This belief prompts us to pray constantly, personally and communally, particularly through the reading of Scripture and devotion to the rosary, especially in the family."[40]

Pope John Paul II has also promoted rosary devotion in his writings, speeches and world touring. In *Familiaris Consortio* he wrote, quoting from Pope Paul VI, "We now desire, as a continuation of the thought of our predecessors, to recommend strongly the recitation of the family rosary. . . . There is no doubt that . . . the rosary should be considered as one of the best and most efficacious prayers in common that the Christian family is invited to recite."[41] Obviously the rosary continues to live on today maintaining a rightful place in the prayer life of the Church.

Summary

Proclamation of the rosary as an important prayer for the Christian faithful continues to be a significant teaching of the Catholic Church in the twentieth century. In fact, the first half of this century was probably the most active time for rosary recitation and for other popular devotions. Following on the heels of Pope Leo XIII and his enormous contribution to the rosary, the official teachings of the Church continued to foster great respect for this special form of prayer.

As the twentieth century began to unfold it was apparent that both old and new understandings of the rosary were present. The myth of the rosary's origin with St. Dominic continued to be found in proclamations by Popes Benedict XV and Pius XI. With the pontificate of Pope Pius XII, however, a new and important concept concerning the rosary began to evolve, the idea of family prayer. In *Ingruentium malorum* Pope Pius speaks of the efficacious use of the rosary in the family setting. The Pope's words were in keeping with the trend initiated in 1942 by Father Patrick Peyton who became internationally known as "The Rosary Priest." Through his Family Theater productions and international rosary crusade the rosary and family prayer became common practices in the typical Roman Catholic household. Father Peyton's expression, "The family that prays together, stays together," became a rallying cry for many of the faithful.

Popes John XXIII and Paul VI introduced new teachings on the rosary while continuing the teachings of their predecessors. For Pope John, the rosary was the universal prayer for all the redeemed. Additionally, he taught that the mysteries of the rosary must have a three-fold purpose: mystical contemplation, intimate reflection and pious intention. Pope Paul also emphasized the importance of the mysteries, saying that the prayers of the rosary were merely an empty shell without the mysteries. For Pope Paul, the mysteries are what gives the rosary its christological orientation, placing it in harmony with the major liturgical celebrations of the Church. Both popes continued to foster the family rosary through writings and support of Father Peyton's rosary crusade.

Most recently the American Catholic Bishops have spoken of the rosary's importance in their pastoral letters. In the 1973 pastoral "Behold Your Mother" the bishops stress the efficacy of the rosary and recommend extension and/or substitution of additional mysteries leading to a better understanding of discipleship. In the 1983 pastoral "The Challenge of Peace" much of the historical teaching on the rosary is summarized while promoting the role of family prayer for all the faithful.

Chapter 5 — Notes

1. Beginning with Pope Benedict XV's encyclical *Fausto appetente die* of June 29, 1921, the Roman pontiffs have published over fifty encyclicals, apostolic exhortations, constitutions and major letters which have centered on rosary devotion.
2. *In Coetu soladium*, letter of Pope Benedict XV to Master General of the Friars Preachers, October 29, 1916. See *Papal Teachings; The Holy Rosary*, trans. Rev. Paul J. Oligny, OFM (Boston: Daughters of St. Paul, 1980), p. 163.
3. *Inclytam ac Perillustrem*, letter of Pope Pius XI to Master General of the Friars Preachers, March 6, 1934, paragraph 1.
4. Letter of Pope Benedict XV to Father C. Beechi, O.P., September 18, 1915. See *Papal Teachings; The Rosary*, p. 161.
5. *Inclytam ac Perillustrem*, paragraph 2.
6. The apparitions of the Blessed Virgin Mary as the Lady of the Rosary occurred between May and October 1917. At that time Mary instructed the three seers that daily recitation of the rosary was the solution to world strife and violence. Chapter 8 of this book gives a detailed description of the Fatima story.
7. *Ingravescentibus malis*, encyclical letter of Pope Pius XI, September 29, 1937, paragraph 1. See *The Papal Encyclicals*, vol 4, ed. Claudia C. Ihm (Raleigh, NC: McGrath Publishing Company, 1981).

8. *Ibid.*, paragraph 13.
9. *Ingruentium malorum*, encyclical letter of Pope Pius XII, September 19, 1951, paragraph 7.
10. *Ibid.*, paragraph 6.
11. *Ibid.*, paragraph 5.
12. *Non sine peculiari*, letter of Pope Pius XII to the assistant director of the Apostleship of Prayer, July 1, 1950.
13. "We have learned," letter of Pope Pius XII to Cardinal Griffin, July 14, 1952. *See Papal Teachings: The Rosary*, p. 202.
14. This expression was coined by Father Peyton at the outset of his rosary ministry. The power of this expression was evident in that it became and still is a trademark of Father Peyton's work.
15. The Congregation of Holy Cross, a community of lay religious and clerics, was founded by Father Basil Moreau in France in 1837. In 1841, Father Edward Sorin, a member of the community, came to America to work for the Bishop of the Diocese of Vincennes. Sorin and his colleagues founded the University of Notre Dame in 1842. Although the Holy Cross community no longer owns Notre Dame its influence there is strong. It is one of the major centers of ministry for the Holy Cross community in the United States.
16. Patrick Peyton, C.S.C., *All For Her* (Hollywood, California: Family Theater Publications, 1973), p. 57.
17. *Ibid.*, 69.
18. Cardinal John Francis O'Hara, C.S.C., was a Holy Cross archbishop of Philadelphia. Father Peyton had a loyal supporter in Cardinal O'Hara as they were from the same heritage and religious community. Through the influence of Cardinal O'Hara, Father Peyton's work gained much influence within the faith community.
19. The designation of Father Peyton as "The Rosary Priest" came about predominantly from his worldwide rosary crusade. Through this crusade the importance of family prayer and the rosary became normative for Roman Catholics.
20. Princess Grace narrated two episodes for Family Theater, "The Nativity" and "The Seven Last Words of Christ."
21. Interview with Father Patrick Peyton, C.S.C., South Bend, Indiana, July 5, 1986.

22. *Grata recordatio*, encyclical letter of Pope John XXIII, September 26, 1959, paragraph 13.
23. *Ibid.*, paragraph 1.
24. *Oecumenicum concilium*, apostolic letter of Pope John XXIII, April 28, 1962, paragraph 3.
25. *Grata recordatio* speaks of how the mysteries of the rosary are an instrumental part of the prayer devotion. Meditation upon these mysteries is a natural outgrowth of this devotion and is really the heart of the rosary itself.
26. *Il religioso convegno*, apostolic letter of Pope John XXIII, September 29, 1961, paragraph 9.
27. *Marialis Cultus*, apostolic exhortation of Pope Paul VI, February 2, 1974, paragraph 7.
28. *Ibid.*, paragraph 8.
29. *Ibid.*, paragraph 12.
30. *Ibid.*, paragraph 6.
31. *Ibid.*, paragraph 8.
32. *Mense maio*, encyclical letter of Pope Paul VI, April 29, 1965, paragraph 14.
33. *Ibid.*, paragraph 5.
34. *Christi Matri*, encyclical letter of Pope Paul VI, September 15, 1966, paragraph 5.
35. *Ibid.*, paragraph 7.
36. Allocation to children of the Living Rosary of Pope Paul VI, May 10, 1964, paragraph 5.
37. Personal letter of Pope Paul VI to Father Patrick Peyton, C.S.C., March 12, 1964.
38. "Behold Your Mother — Woman of Faith," Pastoral Letter on the Blessed Virgin Mary, NCCB, November 21, 1973, paragraph 96.
39. *Ibid.*, paragraph 97.
40. "The Challenge of Peace: God's Promise and Our Response," Pastoral Letter on War and Peace, NCCB, May 3, 1983, paragraph 293.
41. *Familiaris Consortio*, Apostolic Constitution of Pope John Paul II, Nov. 22, 1981, paragraph 61.

Chapter 6
The Rosary and
Artistic Expression

Religious art has been an instrumental facet of Christianity from the time of the Apostles. This is only natural as the human race has expressed itself in artistic forms since the dawn of civilization. Artistic expression has told the saga of human life from prehistoric cave dwelling art through the Renaissance and impressionistic eras to the concept of "modern art." Although styles have certainly changed one common denominator seems evident: all art is expressive of the historical period in which it was created. Social, economic, political and religious factors make each period distinctive and thus these influences are very evident in the differing artistic styles.

Religious art has been a source of beauty and enjoyment, as well as one of conflict during the history of Christianity. How many millions of people have viewed Michelangelo's work in the Sistine Chapel and marveled at its greatness? Countless people have been inspired by artistic expression to come to a deeper personal understanding of God. Most Christians today adorn their homes with some work of art which expresses their belief in Christ and other precepts of the faith. This love of art has not always been in peaceful coexistence within the faith community. The Iconoclast controversy of the eighth and ninth centuries in the East brought open rebellion inside the Church itself. Viewing artistic works, specifically icons, as a violation of the first commandment (Exodus 20:4), the Iconoclasts stripped their church buildings bare. The emperors of the Constantinople-based empire, especially Leo III and Constantine V, were strong supporters of Iconoclast policies, especially since they considered themselves kings of the civilized world while Christ was king of heaven alone. It took the work of St. John of Damascus and Empress Irene in 787 to call a council at Nicaea to adjudicate the problem.[1] The council taught, in support of St. John, that icons should be left in the churches. Although the ninth century saw three additional iconoclastic emperors, the council's work eventually won the battle.

Although the way has not always been smooth it is evident from history that art has touched all facets of Christian belief. The rosary has not been exempt from this outpouring of artistic expression. Rosary art forms seem to follow the evolutionary history of the prayer devotion which has been outlined in previous chapters. The rose garden theme seems to dominate the early forms of rosary art. The legends of St. Dominic, popular in the early Renaissance period, have been the inspiration for numerous works as well. After the foundation of the Rosary Confraternity there seems to be a shift in emphasis to the beads themselves and their association with all Christian worship. Rosary art has taken all forms. Certainly paintings are predominant in those works which have survived but sculpture and altarpieces are also popular expressions.

Early Rosary Art

Before 1400 there is much evidence showing the emphasis, in pictorial art as well as musical hymns, of a relationship between the Lady of the Rose, and more especially the Lady of the Rose Garden, and the *Ave* prayer beads.[2] In these paintings the *rosarium* may be a garden or an arbor or only a hedge of roses. Certain general characteristics are evident in most all of these works. The

Virgin is usually seated, either holding the Child on her lap or beside her. Some scenes depict the Child playing nearby. Sometimes the two are attended by one or more saints, usually female (Sts. Catherine and Dorothy are favorites). Usually Mary and the Child are also attended by angels. There may be *putti* (cherubs), holding a crown over the Virgin's head or playing instruments or offering the child apples or roses. The whole scene will either be painted in a garden or roses may ring the outside of the action depicted.

The rose garden serves as a unifying factor in many artistic works prior to the fifteenth century. It is this sacred enclosure in which the true meaning of Mary's presence can take full hold for both artist and viewer. Although beads were many times not present in these works, it was evident to the viewer, because of the rose garden scene, that the rosary (as then understood) was being proclaimed in the scene. Roses were as much a symbol of the rosary as the fish was a symbol of Christianity itself.

The whole concept of the maypole, the crowning of Mary and similar Marian devotions can be traced back to this period where the rose garden was so emphasized in Marian art. These contemporary customs have been handed down for centuries displaying the truly powerful image which the rose garden had for Christians of the late medieval and early Renaissance periods. Artistic expression of the period suggested that a May bride be enthroned "like a goddess in an arbour."[3] As explained in our historical study of the rosary's development, the bride in such paintings, who is often called a rose, is most probably the Rose of Sharon (Song of Songs), the bride who is also wisdom.[4] Thus the present-day customs of Marian devotion in May have many of their roots in the Wisdom literature of the Hebrew Scriptures.

By the beginning of the fourteenth century, the Paradise Garden, with its roses, is often clearly and intimately associated with the Marian Psalter. Paintings reveal that at least fifty years before the term "rosary" was officially established as meaning both the Marian devotion, and by extension the beads, the connection was recognized in places as widely separated as Flanders, the

Upper Rhenish district and Italy.[5] By the end of the century the Madonna of the Rose Garden was a frequent subject, most especially in Florence.

Although examples abound, two specific works of art illustrate most poignantly how the rose garden theme began to predominate in the art forms expressive of rosary devotion. In his "Paradise Garden," Stefano da Zevio (or da Verona, 1375-1451) has created a masterpiece which truly depicts the importance of the rose garden in Marian devotion. The painting is hedged with a trestle of roses. The Virgin supports the standing child with one arm. In her free hand she holds a rose while gazing toward a book that one assumes is the Psalter. Bird-like angels are perched on the trellis. Some of the angels fly about gathering roses. Two of the angels carry a basket full of roses to a woman seated on a flowing lawn weaving a chaplet of roses. The woman is most probably St. Catherine of Alexandria, the mystic bride of the infant Jesus.

Jan van Eyck's "Virgin of the Fountain" (1439) is equally expressive of this important paradise garden motif. In a garden closed off by a hedge of dark pink roses the Virgin stands on a strip of tapestry, the free end of which is held up behind her, like the back of a throne, by two flying angels. The lawn is dense with lilies-of-the-valley and violets. Additional roses protrude from behind the tapestry, fed by waters from a fountain that stands to the right of the Virgin. The Child in Mary's arms dangles from one hand a tasselled pair of coral beads, the same color as the roses.

Another distinct theme in rose garden art is that drawn between heaven and the earthly paradise of the Lady's rose garden.[6] In the Spanish Chapel of St. Maria Novella in Florence, the Italian artist Andrea (Bonaiuti) da Firenza (1343-1377) has depicted this theme. The painting shows one end of a courtly garden, a rose hedge, and beside it, the gates of heaven. The faithful ready to enter first kneel and are crowned with a chaplet of roses. Giovanni da Fiesole (Blessed Angelico) has also depicted this dichotomy. In a painting dating from approximately 1450 he shows a group of angels as well as saints of his community (Dominicans), some of them wearing chaplets of roses, some singing and some dancing.

All of the people in the painting are proceeding toward a gateway from which the ultimate light streams out. Most probably the dancers on the other side of the gate are the perfected souls who have already passed to everlasting happiness in heaven. Both artists have shown that although the rose garden is a good earthly paradise it is not the goal. The theme that Marian devotion and the rosary are tools to achieve final union with Christ is strong in both of these paintings.

The most important artistic theme of this period was that depicting Mary as the Madonna of the Rose Garden. These works are most famous for their depiction of Mary and her being crowned within the garden itself. Although a fine line separates what works would qualify for this category, certain pieces (including Van Eyck's "Virgin of the Fountain") are unquestionably members of this select field.[7] In "Madonna of the Rose-Arbor," Stephan Lochner (1410-1451) has created what some critics consider the epitome of rose garden art. In this painting the arbor is a jewel-like frail construction lightly wreathed in red roses. Framed in the scene a youthful Virgin stands attired in a blue robe and mantle carrying the child Jesus. She wears a jewelled crown including a pattern of roses, ruby-red and deep sapphire-blue. She is almost totally ringed in by eager and absorbed little angels, most of them making music, one offering Jesus an apple, one picking a rose for him.

An altarpiece by Antonello da Messina (1473) expresses well the madonna theme. The work brings together the enthroned Madonna crowned with roses. The child wears a large twig of coral on a string round his neck together with a chaplet of beads. The simple metal crown held over the Madonna's head by flying angels has entwined in its points pink and white roses. Over the edge of the white marble pedestal just beyond the hem of her rose-pink dress, droops a loose necklace of thirty-eight round blue-black beads.

Additional paintings of the early sixteenth century continue to depict Mary as the Madonna of the Rose Garden. In the "Madonna of the Rose-Bed" an unknown Upper Flemish master has depicted the Virgin seated by a rose hedge handing the Child Jesus a white rose. The scene is surrounded by a border of roses. Another painting by the same artist, circa 1410, entitled the "Little Paradise-Garden" has a low crenelated wall surrounding a rather shaggy carpet of flowers including the traditional lilies of the valley and at the Virgin's feet the violets of humility. Pretty birds including the goldfinch, bullfinch and yellow hammer are present. The Lady sits abstracted, reading what must be the Psalter. Among the courtiers is a golden-haired girl supervising the Child's playing.

"Das Rosenkranzfest" by Albrecht Dürer (1506) exemplifies in many ways all of the themes in rosary devotion popular at the dawn of the sixteenth century.[8] In the center of the painting the Virgin sits holding the Child in her right arm. Chaplets of alternating pink and white roses tightly bound on small wooden hoops are used for notaries. The Madonna crowns the Emperor Maximilian and the Child crowns the pope. Other persons, both lay and clerical, only some of whom carry rosaries, are receiving their rose-chaplets from angels who have supplies slung over their arms. St. Dominic stands at the right hand of the throne, just beyond the Child, crowning the bishop. Two flying angels hold the Virgin's crown above her head while two additional angels hold a green tapestry behind the Lady. This painting shows the importance of roses but in addition the beads themselves are represented. Also, the presence of St. Dominic in the work shows the strong influence of the legends about Dominic and his association with the rosary.[9]

Although the rose garden is the dominant theme, it is not the sole motif used in rosary artistic expression prior to 1500. There are many examples of the rosary in religious art where its presence is historically inconsistent: the rosary did not exist at the time depicted in the scene. In 1484 Hermann Rode was commissioned by the Painter's Confraternity of St. Luke in Lubeck to paint an altarpiece for the local Church of St. Catherine. On one panel Luke the Evangelist is depicted in his study with a chaplet of five octaves hanging from a nail in his closet. Another example is the scene of the Dormitian of the Virgin, a panel of the Geschlachtwander altarpiece. One of the Apostles at the foot of her death bed leans over, holding a chaplet of large wooden beads.

Along with being historically inaccurate, several sacred paintings use the rosary simply as a piece of anachronistic equipment. St. Joseph is many times portrayed as a hermit with the beads in hand. In a Visitation scene (circa 1470-1480) St.Elizabeth wears them.[10] In the "Annunciation" (1497) of Il Borgognone (Ambrogio Fossano, 1450-1523) the beads symbolize the Virgin's contemplative nature. In the painting, located in the Church of the Incoronata at Lodi, near Milan, Mary is depicted as a well-born and pious girl of the painter's time. A five-decade chaplet of coral beads hangs over the back of a leather chair, from which she quietly rises on the entrance of the angel Gabriel. Both in composition and symbolically these coral beads supply a link between the red of Gabriel's cloak and the red of Mary's dress. The intersection of time present and time past is suggested by the scene, which depicts a set of then-contemporary rosary beads and an hour glass resting on a book together with the peacock of immortality in the cortile seen beyond the beads.

In Roger van der Weyden's "Adoration of the Magi" (circa 1455-1460) the rosary, although somewhat anachronistic, places the character who holds it in a particularly powerful position. In a busy scene a little Dutch figure kneels outside a low wall behind St. Joseph with his long pair of coral beads hanging down inside the wall from between his clasped hands. Although seemingly a rather marginal figure in the painting, he may be one of the most important people because of his obvious meditative state.

The rosary has been depicted in numerous paintings with the saints both in fact and legend. Although the concept of a rosary had not yet been developed, St. Antony Abbot and St. Jerome, the well-known hermits, are often depicted with prayer beads in their hands or on their person.[11] Certainly the most popular and well-known saint as a subject for rosary art is St. Dominic. Many distinguished artists including Rubens, Veronese, van Dyck, Murillo and Caravaggio have used St. Dominic as the subject of a painting.[12] Almost always the rosary is present in the scene, generally in a predominant place. The painting by Barocci (1526--1612) in the Ashmolean, Oxford, is a small but powerful painting. The Madonna looms in an accumulation of cloud and draperies.

She drops an invisible chaplet so that it will fall into a scapular held out like an apron by St. Dominic kneeling below. Another remarkably attractive piece, with a quite different treatment of the rosary, is a fresco by Guido Reni (1570-1642), located in the Sanctuary of Our Lady and St. Luke outside Bologna. The painting depicts the mysteries of the rosary on the coin-like leaves of a plant growing out of a vase. This calls to mind the medieval use of the genealogical tree, the Stem of Jesse, the family tree of great Dominicans.[13] Although subtle the Dominican legends are present here as well.

The Rosary and Art Since 1500

After 1500 the theme in religious rosary art took a serious turn toward a more fundamental and basic use of the rosary itself. This was due probably in large measure to the founding of the Rosary Confraternity in Cologne in 1474 (Sprenger's version). As the beads themselves became more predominant in rosary art, so too was there a trend to show the child Jesus with the beads. After 1500 it became quite common to see the Child playing with the beads. Whether the Child wore them, dangled or waved the beads or even if he merely held them out demonstratively to the people, the message seemed clear: use the rosary in prayer. This theme is depicted wonderfully in an altarpiece of 1499 by Hans Holbein the Elder. In this work the child Jesus holds an open string of *Ave* beads outstretched between his hands as angels fly over, holding the Virgin's crown.[14]

The sixteenth century also brought forth a predominant color scheme which became very popular and common to all rosary art forms. White came to signify the purity of the Virgin and was seen to represent all those who pray the joyful mysteries. Red reminded viewers of the heartfelt compassion which Mary held for all people, especially her Son. Those who prayed the sorrowful mysteries were represented by red. Yellow or gold came to symbolize the great joy and jubilation in heaven as Mary ascended above the angelic chorus to heaven. The glorious mysteries were represented by yellow or gold.[15]

The Renaissance was the principal time of history when the arts began to truly flourish. In cooperating with this overflow of artistic expression, rosary art, too, expanded and became a basic element to religious artistic expression. Artists of the sixteenth century forward began to paint the beads into most all religious scenes. Displaying the beads so readily in most all art forms of the day was a natural outpouring from the popularity of the prayer. One of the most popular themes during this period continued a previously used motif, that of the Madonna and Child. With sixteenth century Renaissance art, however, the previously mentioned highlighting of the beads and the new distinctive color scheme were used.[16]

Madonna and Child representations presented the beads in various ways. There did not seem to be any differences in rosary representations based upon the theme of the work. Whether the artistic work was based on biblical and/or historical data or if the work was hieratic or symbolic, the beads seemed to follow no specific pattern in the way they were depicted in the work. The beads may be used decoratively, draped in the background either irregularly or symmetrically, or be used in the festoon arrangement of which the Italian Renaissance painters were so fond. A particularly beautiful and remarkable piece is the "Madonna of Victory" by Andrea Mantegna (1496). Here the beads, arranged in groups of six, are hung like streamers from the apex of a fruit-garlanded and bud-haunted apre-like garden in which the Madonna is enthroned. The pendant of the rosary, terminating in a whole tree of coral, hangs exactly over the Child's head. Matthias Grünewald's "Madonna of the Snow" shows the beads at the edge of the painting, casually spilling out of a bowl. The beads could be worn by the Virgin, the Child, or the Child could play with them. In Il Borgogne's "Madonna and Child," the Child, seated demurely on a little stool, holds a chaplet between both hands while pointing at a book. This book is most probably the Psalter displaying a thematic holdover from the pre-Rosary Confraternity days.

The "Madonna on the Cloud of Angels" by Albrecht Altdorfer (circa 1480-1538) shows an unusual depiction of the beads. In this work the Child holds a large rosary in one hand; the beads rest over his Mother's arm. The Child's free hand is raised in a gesture of preaching or blessing that proves that he is no ordinary child. Here we see a transition between the pre-sixteenth century garden motif and its natural and docile Madonna and Child to a new motif of authority which seems present after the foundation of Blessed Alanus de Rupe's Rosary Confraternity.

The rosary and Mary were present in other artistic works which do not depict the Madonna and Child theme. One of the most spectacular scenes is present in Michelangelo's epic work "The Last Judgment." In this painting Mary is seen drawing into heaven a sinner who is falling into the abyss. She throws her rosary out to him as a rope of safety to which the man clings, frantically summoning all his effort. The scene is very graphic and could easily lead one to believe that Michelangelo felt the rosary was a significant tool in the battle against evil in the world.

Art depicting the saints and the rosary continued to flourish in the sixteenth century as in previous times. Again, however, the emphasis on the beads themselves is most predominant. Contrary to what might be thought, St. Dominic is not featured as prominently in such works. Remember that the Rosary Confraternity, which seems to have aided the shift in rosary art to a more dominant depiction of the beads, was a Dominican institution. Also, as we have seen by the work of St. Louis de Montfort, legends of St. Dominic's role in the rosary story continued to predominate during the sixteenth century and beyond. In fact most European art tended to associate the rosary with nuns, members of knightly orders and lay people as opposed to monks and friars.[17] Women were more predominantly associated with the rosary. This is seen in a painting by Gerard David (died 1523) in which St. Catherine receives her mystic marriage ring while the Child wears, bandoleer style, a loosely strung rosary of glass beads.

Painting was not the only rosary art form which flourished during the Renaissance period. The two best examples of sculpture which represent the rosary motif are German, both being created within a few years of each other. Tilman Riemenschneider's "Madonna in the Rosary," begun in 1521, is the last Madonna work of his for which there is documentation. The piece stands in the choir loft of the Church of St. Mary in a vineyard near Wurzburg. The Virgin is standing with the Child in her arms, with a tapestry-like cape behind her. The scene depicts a garden of fifty stylized roses, overlapping like shingles on a roof and divided by five medallions. The Madonna, with her head slightly tilted, has an unusually withdrawn, almost weary look. Obviously the new emphasis of depicting the beads is missing but the significance in this piece is the accurate depiction of five groups of roses, foreshadowing the basic five decades of the rosary.

Veit Stoss's "Ave Maria" (1517-1519) lies in the Church of St. Lorenz in Nuremberg. The Virgin and Gabriel stand on an angel-borne console that extends to the sides of the garland. Over the scene of the garden of roses, which is interspersed by medal-lions (two extra medallions act like helium balloons to buoy the garland up), a pair of beads is poised with six decades over against the five decades of the garland.

The altarpiece was also used to express devotion to the rosary. An altarpiece commissioned in 1475 to commemorate the found-ing of the Rosary Confraternity stands in Cologne. The present painting is a remake from sometime in the sixteenth century. Apparently the original version had a frame of fifty stylized *Ave* roses divided by five *Pater* roses. The two outermost panels, St. Dorothy left and St. Cecilia right, were exterior, closing over St. Dominic and St. Peter Martyr so that the Madonna was flanked, when the retable was shut, by two maids-in-waiting. Dorothy and Cecilia are both associated by legend with rose garlands. The Madonna stands with the Child seated upright, steadied by her right arm. The Virgin stands as the Lady of the Mantle of Mercy, under which members of the Confraternity kneel for protection. In a dual role the Virgin also is presented as the Queen of the Rosary. She is wearing round her neck a long rosary of coral *Ave* beads and agate *Pater* beads, including three enamel beads serving as the pendant. The Child in the scene is playing with the beads.

Three additional altarpieces are of significant note in the history of religious rosary art. A work completed by Michael and Martin Zirn (circa 1640) stands in Uberlingen on Lake Constance. The piece has a tremendously gilded free-standing Madonna poised in an oval of mystery medallions that are linked by chaplets of beads. The figures of St. Francis and St. Dominic are present in the work. In an altarpiece in St. Domenico in Bologna (circa 1640) an elaborately decorated frame of gilded wood stands within a frame of fifteen panels depicting the mysteries. The Madonna is shown enthroned with the Child in her lap. The Virgin has two rosaries round her neck; the child dangles a third rosary. The third rosary altarpiece, by Sassoferrato (1605-1685), stands in the rosary chapel of St. Sabina in Rome. St. Dominic and St. Catherine are shown kneeling on marble steps at the feet of the enthroned Madonna who is mantled in blue, as prescribed by the art censor of the Holy See after the Council of Trent.[18] Both saints carry lilies of chastity and a garland of sumptuous roses. Dominic receives a rosary from the Virgin; Catherine receives her beads from the child Jesus.

Summary

There is certainly no doubt that religious art has played a significant role in the advancement and promotion of the faith. Despite the period of Iconoclasm in the East, art has survived to aid the Christian faithful in their daily challenge to follow Christ. The rosary has been a significant and long-lasting theme in sacred art. Paintings, sculptures and altarpieces highlight the spectrum of visual art which promotes the rosary and its devotion.

Before the fifteenth century the principal theme of sacred rosary art was the image of the rose garden, the Psalter and Mary's association with same. Most of the artistic works of this period dealing with the rosary pictured the Virgin, generally with Child, in a rose garden or arbor. Chaplets of roses were also very predominant in many of these works. "The Paradise Garden," exemplified by the mastery of Stefano da Zevio, was a central theme to many of the paintings. Association with Mary's Psalter led one to enjoy the paradise of this earth which would translate, as depicted by Bonaiuti, into the paradise of everlasting life. The Madonna of the Rose Garden was a second major theme of this pre-Renaissance rosary art. This motif became very popular and was translated by such artists as Stephan Lochner and Antonello da Messina into works which foreshadowed the famous "Madonna and Child" of the Renaissance period. Here again the rose garden environment was very much a part of the scene.

The rose garden motif was also seen in rosary works which were not associated with Mary. Biblical scenes and pictures of saints who lived before Dominic began to display the chaplet of beads and/or roses in their expression. Although these scenes were obviously contrived (as the rosary did not exist in biblical times) the point was clear: the rosary and its association with the rose garden had become an important theme for Christians. Scenes with St. Dominic and other saints were popular. The message was still the same —use the rosary as a prayer aid leading to salvation.

A transition occurred in rosary art near the dawn of the sixteenth century. At this time the depiction of the beads themselves became predominant in the art form. Additionally, a specific color scheme is found which delineates the mysteries of the rosary. The primary theme found in Renaissance rosary art was the motif of the Madonna and Child. This form is similar to the Paradise Garden of previous periods but with emphasis on the beads. The Madonnas of Grünewald and Altdorfer are very representative of this style. The new emphasis on the beads carried over to art forms other than painting. Both in works of sculpture and the specific form of the altarpiece, rosary art was prevalent and noteworthy. Altarpieces in Germany showed a great advance in the understanding of the rosary. Decades of rosary beads were seen in those works, plus panels representing the fifteen mysteries. Consistent with official recognition of this prayer devotion, rosary art began to depict the prayer in the physical format that we recognize today.

Sacred rosary art has developed alongside the prayer's devotion. Starting from a basic theme of the rose garden and Marian Psalter, rosary art had progressed by the mid-sixteenth century to depict the rosary, with its mysteries, in a form very close to that used today. In so doing, sacred rosary art has helped promote the prayer and thereby assist Christians in their struggle to live their daily vocation to holiness.

Chapter 6 — Notes

1. Empress Irene, leader of the Constantinople-based empire, called the council at Nicaea to give official voice to St. John's work. John had died in 749 but his work was not forgotten. See *The Christian Faith*, ed. J. Neuner, S.J., and J. Dupuis, S.J., article 1251. The Nicaea II Council declared, "We define that . . . the representatives of the precious and life-giving cross, and the venerable and holy images as well . . . must be kept in the holy Church of God."
2. Artistic representations of the rosary and its associated rose garden and/or arbor were consistent with the development of the prayer devotion. Thus, prior to the fifteenth century the rose garden was a strong theme in art depicting the Marian Psalter.
3. This popular theme was an outgrowth of reflection upon the Song of Songs in Hebrew Scripture, especially the first Dialogue of the Bride and Bridegroom (Songs 1:12-2:7).
4. See Songs 2:1-2.
5. Paintings by Jan van Eyck, "Virgin of the Fountain," Stefano da Zevio, "Paradise-Garden," and Stephan Lochner are examples of the widespread attraction of the paradise garden theme in art.
6. The contrast between heaven and earth has been a common

theme in the life of Christians since apostolic times. This is seen most vividly in St. Paul's famous eschatological verses in II Thessalonians, I Corinthians and Galatians.

7. As will be described, there is a fine line difference between the Madonna of the Rose Garden of pre-sixteenth century art and the Madonna and Child theme popular at the height of the Renaissance. Distinctive coloring and the presence of the beads in the scene are more representative of the high Renaissance period.

8. Important themes of the period depicted in this painting include roses, the beads, Church-state association and the use of the rosary by the faithful.

9. As described extensively in chapter 2, the apocryphal accounts of St. Dominic's association with the rosary were very popular during this period, even to the point of having popes write of Dominic's role in founding the devotion.

10. In the Visitation found in the altarpiece of the Virgin (circa 1470) by the Master of the Life of Mary (Munich), a long string of beads, arranged in groups of four, is round about her waist with a pendant falling to one side reaching below the knee.

11. "St. Jerome in the Desert" by Bono da Ferrara (circa 1440), on permanent loan to the National Gallery in Washington, D.C., is an example of such a depiction.

12. See Winifred Kirsch, *Handbuch des Rosenkranzes* (Vienna: Dom-Verlag, 1950), especially pp. 25-35.

13. The Dominicans, along with other religious communities, trace their heritage through a genealogical style tree showing by chronology the great men and women of their order.

14. The altarpiece, although not as prominent as painting, was a significant contributor to rosary art. This piece is found in the Germanisches National Museum in Nuremberg.

15. The colors used, white for the joyful mysteries, red for the sorrowful mysteries and gold for the glorious are in keeping with the colors used in liturgical celebration of the Roman Catholic Church today.

16. See note 7. The prominent place of the beads and the color scheme adopted by the Council of Trent for sacred art were

important factors in Renaissance rosary art.

17. This conclusion is drawn from a representative review of the rosary art of the period. Since, as we have seen, the rosary was developed as a means for the laity to pray in common with the clergy, it is natural that non-clerical peoples be highlighted in rosary art.

18. In session twenty-five of the Council of Trent (1563), decrees were published supporting the Nicaea II Council (see note 1). As a follow-on to the Council's work the Holy See prescribed a certain color scheme to be used in all sacred art sponsored by the Vatican.

Chapter 7
Prayer Beads in World Religions

Our emphasis in this book has been the development of the Christian rosary throughout history. As alluded to in the introduction, however, Christianity is not the only great world religion to use prayer beads for praise and celebration. In the scope of world history, Christianity was the last (development of prayer counters in Islam was coincident with Christianity) great religion to begin use of some form of prayer counting system. It is impossible to prove that the Christian rosary developed totally independently from eastern influence. The development which has been traced in this book could have been influenced by the powerful religious culture present in India. We know that radiations from India's religious cult were found in China and in countries to the West.[1] As noted earlier it is evident that the Christian prayer counting system was being used by the thirteenth century in its own development. Although the Christian system was independently developed for its own specific use, it is still possible that influence from eastern caravans and other contacts may have given more purpose to the development of a counting system.

The origin of the eastern rosary (one can only really speak of the term *rosary* when speaking of Christian worship, but the term succinctly and accurately conveys the idea of prayer beads) is even less traceable than that of Christianity. The first acknowledged evidence for some form of religious prayer counter is in a stone bas-relief at Nineveh dating from the ninth century B.C.E.[2] This artifact shows two winged female figures standing before a sacred tree in an attitude of worship. Each carries in its left hand something that looks like a rosary of today. Scholars differ as to whether this is intended as a garland or prayer beads.[3] For what it is worth, this is the earliest suggestion of rosaries found among the Assyrian peoples. In the Far East many representations of different deities including Brahma, Seva and Kwan Yin carry rosary-like ornaments on their person. However, it is difficult to establish dates older than the ninth century B.C.E. artifacts of Assyria.[4]

Hinduism

It is generally agreed that of the three great non-Christian world religions which use some form of rosary, Hinduism, Buddhism and Islam, the use of beads appears first among the Hindus. Hinduism is a prehistoric religion whose first scriptures are a set of four hymns called Vedas, the earliest of which dates from about 1000 B.C.E.[5] These writings present a multitude of gods but they were later interpreted as revealing a single underlying spirit which moved through the whole universe including humankind. The spirit was given the name Brahm. Since ordinary people could not expect to grasp the abstract notions of the Brahm, the priests, known as Brahmins, compiled voluminous books of detailed observance. These texts made their appearance about 800 B.C.E. and were called Brahmanas. It is in these brahminical writings that we find the first clear mention of the Hindu rosary.[6]

In order to understand the Hindu use of prayer beads we must understand one of the important developments of the brahminical teaching. As the Brahmins purified the old Vedas of their many gods and focused on the abstract spirit, the people longed for the warmth of a personal, concrete god. Therefore, two deities, Siva and Visnu, were reunited from the old legends. Worship of these two gods has formed the two main divisions of Hinduism ever since. Each god is worshiped by its devotees as supreme, and Brahma (the active counterpart of Brahm) takes a lesser place as an emanation of the chosen god.[7] High-caste Brahmins use prayer beads as a means to count prayers, while ascetics use them to further personal contemplation. The common Hindu man or woman uses the beads to count repetitions of the names and epithets of the deity. The number of beads and their material of construction varies with each sect.

Followers of the god Siva use a prayer counter of thirty-two (or sixty-four) beads made from the rough seeds of the rubraksa tree.[8] This seed is grooved; the number of grooves or facets has devotional and ritual significance. The most common number of facets is five, which is said to represent the five faces of Siva. Celibate yogis wear beads made of seeds with eleven facets; those of married yogis have two facets. Legend says that the seeds themselves are tears of Siva which the god shed in anger and crystallized in this fashion.

Those Hindus who follow Visnu prefer the smooth seeds of the tulasi tree, sacred to Visnu.[9] There are 108 beads in this rosary format. These prayer beads are used in an initiation ceremony which children undergo at the age of six or seven years. The beads are placed around the child's neck when the child is taught some sacred formula or sentence. There is a rosary known as the Flag of Visnu consisting of five gems produced from the five elements of nature: sapphire from the earth, pearl from the water, ruby from fire, topaz from air, and diamond from the ether or space.

Other practices are seen in the Hindu use of prayer beads. The Sikhs use a rosary of 108 knots instead of beads. Additionally, this sect of Hinduism can use iron beads, especially a rosary of twenty-seven beads worn on the wrist. The Jain sect, considered by some Hindus to be a separate religion,[10] have rosaries of five different colors, each with its own significance and purpose. Many Hindus attach much importance to the size of the beads. They believe that the larger they are, the more efficacious and meritorious will be their prayers. Superstition exists in the Hindu religion on losing rosary beads. In a Brahminist monastery a novice is warned against losing his beads. If the beads are lost then the novice is allowed no food or drink until the beads are found or he has been invested by the superior with a new rosary.

Hindu rosary edification varies in its practice. In being edified the name of Siva or Visnu is mentally recited with attention being abstractly fixed on the attribute or character conjured up by the verbal recitation of the name.[11] Others, like the popular Hare Krishna sect in the United States, stir their devotion through repetitious voicing of the chant, "Hare, Krishna, Krishna, Krishna, Hare, Hare, Hare, Ram."[12] Although its use is much different than in the Christian form, Hindu prayer beads do serve a positive function within the context of the prayer practices of this religion.

Buddhism

In Buddhism we find the widest diffusion of the rosary in its varied and complicated forms. Prayer beads in Buddhist countries enjoy application in general use second only to that found in the Roman Catholic Church. This is ironic in that the use of all ritual practices is contrary to the primitive teaching of the Buddha.[13]

Buddhism began in India in the sixth century B.C.E. A Hindu of the warrior caste left wife, child, home and all possessions to seek truth. He first tried the fasts and austerities of the ascetics but decided that there was no more enlightenment to be found in self-mortification than in a life of luxury. Therefore, he sat down under a Bo or Bohdi tree, the Tree of Wisdom, until he found enlightenment. When he arose he had all the answers including the meaning of existence, the cause of sorrow and the way in which release from sorrow might be achieved. All of his doubts were eliminated; he had attained enlightenment and entered Nirvana. He became a Buddha, meaning an enlightened one.

The man stayed in the forest four weeks following his enlightenment. He went forth to spread truth, asking people to give up all the ideas of asceticism that had been associated with religion in India. All the people's previous conceptions about gods, ritual and the development of the soul had to be changed. People had to give up the concept of self-identity, ridding themselves of the idea of "I am." According to the Buddha, what holds humans together, giving us a false sense of individuality, is a set of five forms of togetherness. These forms must be shed by the human to win complete freedom from self and enter enlightenment, Nirvana.[14]

This teaching has undergone immense change over the centuries. The man who was against all gods is now adored as a god by millions of followers who also worship large numbers of lesser Buddhas. This evolution in teaching has brought ritual practice to Buddhism, including the use of prayer beads for worship.

It is evident that the Buddhists derived their prayer beads from the form used in the various Hindu sects. This fact is most evident in their use of a rosary with 108 beads, by the Sanskrit formula used by Buddhists in praying the beads and by certain archeological evidence.[15] The Buddhists use the beads to count repetitions of mystic formulae. The number 108 is significant in many ways for the Buddhist faith. There are:

— 108 mental conditions or sinful inclinations to overcome
— 108 Brahmins summoned at Buddha's birth to foretell his destiny
— 108 volumes of Kahgyur, Tibetan sacred writing
— 108 columns in the White Pagoda of Peking
— 108 welcome fires in Japan on the Feast of the Dead
— 108 rupees usually given in alms
— 108 blows given as punishment in China[16]

A variety of formulae exist for the recitation of the beads which focus on the above themes. They all conclude, however, with the traditional phrase, *Om Mani Padme hum* ("Om, the jewel in the lotus, Hail!").[17]

Although the traditional rosary of 108 beads is most common, there are examples of other forms within Buddhism. The Buddhist Lamas (priests) use a rosary with 108 beads that has an additional provision in its construction for counting the number of times the circle has been made. Often additional attachments of various kinds are present with the standard 108 beads. The form of the beads is quite variable throughout the northern Buddhist nations. Some of the poorest people satisfy themselves with a string of only thirty or forty beads. The most common materials used for the beads are wood, pebbles or bones. More costly materials such as turquoise, coral, amber, silver or even pearls or gems are sometimes used. Authorities say that a rosary made from the bones of some holy Lama is prized above all others.[18]

A survey of the prayer bead utilization in different northern Buddhist nations shows that practice varies not only according to taste or wealth but also in relation to sect, position and ritual significance. In Tibet almost everyone carries a rosary. It is used not only for prayer but also for ordinary counting in business and commerce. The most widely used form is divided into four groups of twenty-seven by three larger beads. The two ends of the string are passed through three extra beads before being knotted. These latter beads are called retainers as they keep the rosary in position and indicate the completion of a cycle. While the laity use beads of any material or color, the Lamas vary their beads, attaching special importance to the color which should correspond to the complexion of the god or goddess being worshipped. Thus, as Thurston states, "A devotee of the goddess Tara, who is of blush green complexion, would use a turquoise rosary; a worshiper of Tam-diri would use a red rosary."[19]

In Korea the Buddhist rosary has 110 beads. The two extra beads are large ones, one at the beginning and one dividing the total count of 108 in two parts. Every bead on the string has its own name. In using the beads, the Korean repeats the phrase, "Om, thou Jewel in the Lotus, Hail,"[20] holding each bead till the person has counted a required number. When the rosary is completed each person repeats, "Oh, the thousand myriad miles of emptiness, the place which is in the midst of the tens of hundreds myriads of emptiness, eternal desert where the true Buddha exists. There is eternal existence with tranquil peace."[21] Korean Buddhists also use a smaller set of beads which they believe if used each day in the four positions of going forth, staying home, sitting and lying down, will allow them to see the land of blessing in their hearts. Intrinsic value is also placed on the material from which the beads are made.

In the Chyei Syek classic we read: "Now you can calculate that in repeating the rosary once you will obtain tenfold virtue. If the beads are of lotus seeds you will obtain blessing a thousandfold. If the beads are of pure crystal you will obtain blessings ten thousandfold. But if the beads are made from the Bohdi tree, even if you only grasp the rosary, the blessing you obtain will be incalculable."[22]

In Japan, the Buddhist rosary reaches its most complicated form and is used by all sects. In the time of St. Francis Xavier, a native convert, Paul of the Holy Faith, described the use of prayer beads in his country: "The whole nation prays on the beads as we do. Those who can read use little books, and those who pray on the beads say on each bead a prayer twice as long as the *Pater Noster*. These strings of beads or rosaries have 108 beads. They say that learned men teach that each man has 108 sorts of sin and that he must say a prayer against each of these."[23] In contemporary Japan the Buddhist prayer beads consist of a string of 112 beads. The ends of the string before being knotted are drawn through two parent beads which have a third opening for this purpose. The upper parent bead stands for the father, sun or Buddha, the lower parent bead represents the mother, moon or Bo, the divine spirit which perfected the enlightenment of the Buddha. From the upper parent bead extend two pendant strings or counters.

The number of prayers may vary and the apparatus used in prayer recitation can become quite complex. In a thoroughly fascinating analysis J. M. James gives the following details of a complicated Japanese rosary used by the Jo-do sect of Buddhism:

> The manipulation during prayer is as follows: using it with either hand, the string which has the forty beads on it is placed with its Oya-dama [parent bead] lying over the first joint of the forefinger, with the other fingers lying through the rosary. It is then turned by the thumb one bead at a time, from the Oya-dama one bead for each prayer, until the Oya-dama comes round to its starting point. The other string, which has fifty-five beads on it, is placed between the second and third fingers of the same hand, and used as the first set of counters. Thus, after one round of the upper rosary has been completed, one bead of the lower rosary is slipped through between the fingers — also from the Oya-dama — and so on, one

bead for every round of the upper rosary, until the whole of the lower rosary has been exhausted, when recourse is had to one of the small pendant beads to indicate the fact. The whole process has then to be gone through over again, so that by the time the whole of the sixteen counters have been once used, 35,200 prayers have been recited. This style of double rosary was first introduced by Awanosuke, one of the personal attendants of the founder of this sect, the intention being that it should be manipulated only with the left hand, thus leaving the right hand free for waiting on and carrying out the orders of his superior.[24]

Chinese Buddhists share many of the traditions of the Japanese form just outlined. In China the rosary consists of 108 beads, the same mystic number as with its religious neighbors. Variations to the norm of 108 beads do exist but are rare. Before the communist takeover of mainland China in 1949, rosary beads were very much a part of the normal life of the people.[25] The Chinese official necklace, formerly worn by dignitaries on state occasions, is the Buddhist rosary made into a part of the court costume. In contemporary Chinese society the use of prayer beads has diminished (as is true in Catholicism) but the roots for their use in eastern society is still very much a fact of history.

Islam

Muhammadism or Islam was born in the Near East in the seventh century after Christ. Islam's chief prophet, Muhammad, was enlightened to the ways of Allah; he attracted many proselytes in a short amount of time. The religion is based on submission of one's will and actions to the will of Allah. The word Islam itself is the infinitive of the Arabic verb "to submit." The members of the faith call themselves Muslims or Moslems from the past participle of the same verb, meaning "those who have submitted themselves."[26]

The sacred word of Islam is the Koran, which is said to have been revealed to Muhammad page-by-page during the now sacred month of Ramadan. The book is a somewhat repetitious and difficult-to-read mixture of the Hebrew Scriptures, New Testament and overtones of the former religions of Arabia. The major holy city for Islam is Mecca with its cube-shaped shrine, the Kaaba, which shelters the Black Stone associated with Allah.

Historically it appears that the prophet Muhammad was rejected by both the Jewish and Christian lines of faith and only then did he found his own community of belief. At first Muhammad was persecuted by the people of Mecca. In the year 622 he fled to the city of Medinah for refuge. The flight is called the Hegira and the chronology of the Muslim faith dates from that year. In Medinah, Muhammad formed around him a band of fanatical (fighting) followers. He began a series of raids on caravans and ultimately took the city of Mecca in 630. By the treaty that followed, Mecca was to worship only Allah and accept Muhammad as his prophet. All followers of the new faith were required to make a pilgrimage to Mecca.[27]

Muslims are not much given to discussion of the nature of God. The duties of members are relatively simple and consist of what have been called the five pillars of Islam: the Kalimah, or profession of faith, prayer, almsgiving, fasting and pilgrimages.[28] The Kalimah, which need only be recited with full conviction and understanding once in a lifetime, is "There is no God except Allah; Muhammad is His Prophet."[29] Certain passages from the Koran usually follow this basic statement. The dogmas they include have been summed up as: I believe in Allah, His angels, His books and His messengers, the Last Day, the resurrection from the dead, predestination by God, good and evil, the judgment, the balance, paradise and Hell-fire.[30]

The remaining four pillars of Islam all contribute to the overall submission of the self. Prayer must be made five times per day: morning, noon, afternoon, evening and night, and must be preceded by ablutions which may be made, if water cannot be obtained, by sand. The noon prayer on Friday, the sacred holy day of Islam, is a public service in the mosque. Almsgiving asks that all Muslims give not less than a fortieth of their goods to the poor.[31] The great Muslim fast is the whole month of Ramadan, during which eating and drinking are forbidden in the daytime, though nourishment may be taken at night.

From this summary of the practices of Islam it is obvious that prayer is a major part of the everyday life of all Muslims. Since the prayer of Islam consists chiefly of multiple repetitions of brief phrases, the development of some sort of prayer counter was natural. As described in the introduction, it seems apparent that a parallel development of prayer counters occurred within the faiths of Christianity and Islam. Although both prayer counters were developed to fill a basic need of counting, the similarity between the two systems stops there.

The Muhammadan rosary, called subha or tasbih, consists of ninety-nine beads for reciting the ninety-nine names or attributes of Allah plus a hundredth bead called the leader or Imam. The rosary is also used for counting repetitions of prayers known as the takbir (Allah is very great), the tasbih (I extol Allah), the tahmid (Allah be praised) and the tahlil (There is no deity but Allah). The significance attached to these prayers is indicated in the belief, "Whoever recites this sentence [the tasbih and the tahmid] a hundred times morning and evening, will have his sins forgiven."[32]

Most historians reject the legend which traces the use of the beads back to Muhammad. Beads are mentioned as a novelty more than 200 years after the prophet's death. One Muslim sect, the Wahhabis, count their prayers on their fingers because their founder considered the rosary an abomination not sanctioned by the Koran.

E. W. Lane has described one use of the Muhammadan rosary from the late nineteenth century. On the night following the death and burial of a man, a large number of fakirs assembled at the deceased's home, one carrying a large rosary of 1,000 beads. During the prayer service some passages of the Koran were recited. Then the formula, "There is no deity but Allah" was repeated 3,000 times. One of the fakirs kept count by means of the rosary. When the full 3,000 repetitions were completed one of the fakirs asked his companions, "Have you transferred [the merit of] what you have recited to the soul of the deceased?" They replied, "We have transferred it," and added, "and peace be on all the Apostles, and praise be to Allah, the Lord of all creatures."[33]

Various materials are used in Muhammadan rosaries. Date stones are popular, as is wood. Other more costly materials may be used; each sect tends to migrate toward a particular material. The ninety-nine beads are generally divided into three equal groups, usually by a bead of a different shape, but sometimes by tassels, called *shamsas*, of gold thread or silk of various colors.[34]

Summary

The use of prayer beads is not an exclusively Christian phenomenon. In fact, history shows us that, of the great world religions, Christianity was probably the last to formally use some means of counting for repetitive prayers. Origins of some evidence of religious prayer counting can be found as far back as the ninth century before Christ in the culture of Assyria. Although little is known or can be determined from the scant evidence of the period, it is evident that some system of counting religious incantations has been present in society for nearly three millennia.

It is generally agreed that of the three great non-Christian world religions which use prayer counters, the beads first appeared among the Hindus. In the Brahminical writings of the ninth century B.C.E. we find the first clear mention of a Hindu rosary. Based on the resurrection of two old legend gods, Siva and Visnu, two different forms of Hindu rosary devotion came into practice. Followers of Siva used a prayer counter of thirty-two or sixty-four beads, each with five facets representing the five faces of Siva. Followers of Visnu used a rosary of 108 beads. For both groups the beads served as counters for the mental prayer which focused upon some attribute or character of the god being remembered. This is seen in such repetitive prayers as used by the presently popular Hare Krishna sect in the United States and other nations.

In Buddhism we find the widest diffusion of the rosary in many complicated and varied forms. It seems evident that Hindu influence was strong in the Buddhists' use of prayer beads. Buddhists use a rosary of 108 beads, on which are remembered the important mysteries of their faith, all of which have the number 108 involved with their character. Although formulae differ, all incantations using the beads end with the traditional phrase, "Om, the Jewel in the Lotus, Hail." Surveying the use of prayer beads in northern Buddhist nations it is evident that besides personal preference and wealth, the practice of rosary use is also affected by relation to sect, position and ritual significance. Additionally, the color of the rosary used by the Lamas (priests) signifies the god being worshiped in the prayer devotion.

Buddhist practices in Korea, Japan and China are each unique. In Korea a rosary of 110 beads is most predominant. Each bead has its own name. Reciting the proper prayer in the proper position each day will allow one to see the land of blessing in the person's heart. Intrinsic value is placed on the material from which the beads are made. In Japan a very complicated form of rosary is used. The number of prayers and the apparatus used can become so complex that a full recitation of the beads could total more than 35,000 prayers. Chinese Buddhists share many of the same traditions of the Japanese. The rosary consists of 108 beads, the same mystic number used by the Japanese Buddhists. Although severely curtailed in recent years because of the communist influence, prayer beads have been an important concept in Chinese society for centuries.

Islam's use of prayer beads seems to have developed along different but parallel lines to the Christian rosary. In the ninth century, approximately 200 years after the death of Muhammad, Muslims began to use prayer beads as a significant part of their daily devotional life. Using a rosary of ninety-nine beads, Islam recounts the names and attributes of Allah. Also repetitious prayers known as the takbir, tasbih, tahbid and tahlil are prayed many times during the five-fold daily prayer incantations.

It is important to realize that only when we make the word rosary equivalent to the word prayer-counter can we speak of any correlation between Asian and Christian rosaries. In anything but the superficial meaning of the term, there is no relationship at all between the universal Christian method of prayer which is the rosary and the use of beads in other religions. To Christians the rosary is vastly more than a means of counting prayers. It is a tradition-distilled essence of Christian devotion in which vocal and mental prayer unite the whole person in effective and purposeful meditation on the central mysteries of Christian belief. The rosary thus joins the human race to God through Mary whom God chose from all time for the specific purposes of mother and intercessor.

Chapter 7 — Notes

1. Marshall Broomhall, *Islam in China* (London: Morgan and Scott, LTD, 1910), especially pp. 39-60.
2. J. G. Shaw, *The Story of the Rosary* (Milwaukee: The Bruce Publishing Company, 1954), p. 146. B.C.E. refers to "Before the Common Era," a universally accepted term, acceptable to all religions. The designations are equivalent to the common B.C. usage.
3. *Ibid.*
4. *Ibid.*
5. Sir Monier Monier-Williams, *Hinduism* (London: Society for Promoting Christian Knowledge, 1878), p. 19.
6. *Ibid.*, especially pp. 33-38.
7. Sir Monier Monier-Williams, *Brahmanism and Hinduism* (London: John Murray Albemarle Street, 1891), pp. 54-87.
8. *Ibid.*, p. 67.
9. *Ibid.*
10. Sir Monier Monier-Williams, *Hinduism*, pp. 221-23. Monier-Williams points out that Jainism is really akin to Buddhism in its two principal sects of Suetambaras and Digambaras.
11. With such a system there is no definitive pattern of what prayers are said on what beads. This prayer is very spontaneous and is difficult to define. The many attitudes of Siva

or Visnu can be recited in any order.

12. Shaw, *Rosary*, p. 149.

13. For Buddhists, ritual is incompatible with the basic beliefs of the Buddha. The four truths of suffering, cause, cessation and true path and the six principles of causation, indeterminism of the undifferentiated, reciprocal identification, true reality, totality and perfect freedom are common to all schools of Buddhism. Although ritual is practiced as ceremony it is not in keeping with the dictates of Buddha.

14. The concept of Nirvana in Buddhism is somewhat analogous to the Christian concept of heaven. For Buddhists, however, Nirvana can be attained in our present human existence. The original Buddha entered enlightenment, Nirvana, by shedding himself of the concept of "I am." People have great difficulty defining precisely what Nirvana is and how it is attained.

15. L. A. Waddell, *The Buddhism of Tibet* (Cambridge, England: W. Heffer & Sons, LTD, 1934), pp. 202-12.

16. Shaw, *Rosary*, p. 150.

17. *Ibid.*

18. The Buddhist holy person, the Lama, is honored as the spiritual leader of the people. It is thought that the Lama has come closest to achieving Nirvana. Thus, even in death the body of the Lama is highly respected and considered sacred.

19. Herbert Thurston, S.J., "The History of the Rosary in all Countries," *Journal of the Society of Arts* (February, 1902), p. 63.

20. Shaw, *Rosary*, p. 152.

21. *Ibid.*

22. *Ibid.*, pp. 152-53.

23. Orazio Torsellino, *The Admirable Life of St. Francis Xavier*, English Recusant Literature Series, vol. 299, ed. D. M. Rogers (London: The Scholar Press, 1976), p. 263.

24. J. M. James, "The Rosary in Japan," *Transactions of the Asiatic Society of Japan*. See Shaw, *Rosary*, pp. 153-54.

25. The Buddhist population of China used their beads in both religious and social situations. Because of their association with some form of worship, the Communists outlawed their use.

26. Islam is based on the total submission of the self to Allah. Islam, like Christianity and Judaism, is monotheistic and looks upon patriarchal figures such as Moses and Abraham as forebears in faith.

27. The once-per-lifetime pilgrimage to Mecca is still practiced within Islam. Mecca, along with Medinah and Jerusalem (site of the assumption of Muhammad) serve as the holy cities in Islam.

28. F. A. Klein, *The Religion of Islam* (London: Curzon Press, 1971), pp. 37-111.

29. Khurshid Ahmad, "Islam: Basic Principles and Characteristics," *Islam: Its Meaning and Message*, ed. Khurshid Ahmad (London: Islamic Council of Europe, 1976), p. 29.

30. Muhammed Asad, "The Spirit of Islam," *Islam: Its Meaning and Message*, especially pp. 48-55.

31. It is thought that the Muslim custom of giving a fortieth of their goods to the poor was taken from the Judeo-Christian concept of tithing, which the Bible mentions in forty-six different places.

32. Shaw, *Rosary*, pp. 156-57.

33. E. W. Lane, *Manners and Customs of the Modern Egyptians* (London: Dent Publishing Company, 1908), pp. 486-87.

34. Shaw, *Rosary*, pp. 157-58.

Chapter 8
The Message of Fatima

It is certainly evident that the single most revelatory and important event concerning the promotion of the rosary during our century is the series of apparitions of our Lady to three peasant children in Fatima, Portugal in 1917. The significance of these events cannot be overstressed. At Lourdes, Mary had appeared to Bernadette Soubirous with a rosary wrapped in her hands, yet her message to the French farm girl did not concern the rosary.[1] At Fatima, however, the Blessed Virgin acknowledged herself as the Lady of the Rosary. Her message was simple, straightforward and powerful: Pray the rosary each day for world peace. Although Pope Leo XIII's message was clear, the power and influence of the rosary did not become fully clear in this century until Fatima. One may question the timing and logistics of the apparitions (World War I had engulfed Europe, but Portugal was a neutral nation) but the fact remains that Mary's presence and message at Fatima gave the best and most practicable reason for recitation of the rosary, a prayer practiced in Catholicism for close to 500 years.

Apparitions of the Angel of Peace

Although the apparitions of the Virgin Mary occurred in 1917, the story of Fatima and its rosary message actually begins in 1916. The village of Fatima and the even smaller community of Aljustrel are located in a rural agricultural area about 120 miles north of Lisbon. Lucia dos Santos and her two cousins Francisco and Jacinta Marto would daily tend the sheep which their parents raised on their meager farms. One day the children were playing "pebbles" in the Loca do Cabeco, a rock fissure near Aljustrel. To the children's amazement a mysterious apparition appeared to them in a driving wind. Lucia described the scene: "We saw a young man about fourteen or fifteen years old, whiter than snow, transparent as crystal when the sun shines through it, and of great beauty."[2] On reaching them (the young man came to them from above an olive tree) he said, "Do not be afraid! I am the Angel of Peace. Pray with me."[3] Kneeling on the ground, he bowed until his forehead touched the ground and repeated these words three times: "My God, I believe, I adore, I trust and I love You! I ask pardon of You for those who do not believe, do not adore, do not trust and do not love You."[4] Suddenly the young man rose and drifted off to the east. The children agreed to keep the angel's appearance a secret.

Later in the summer, the angel appeared to the children a second time while they played in the garden of Lucia's home. The angel exhorted the children: "Pray, pray very much. Make everything you can a sacrifice and offer it to God as an act of reparation for the sins by which He is offended and in supplication for the conversion of sinners. . . . Above all, accept and bear with submission the suffering which the Lord will send you."[5] Although the angel's words were somewhat ominous and fear-filled the children again agreed to keep these apparitions a secret.

In the late summer of 1916 the angel appeared to the children again at the Loca do Cabeco, the site of the first vision. At the time the children were praying in repetition the first prayer which the angel had recited when an extraordinary light shone upon them. As they looked up they saw the angel with a chalice in his left hand and a host above it in his right from which drops of blood dripped into the chalice. Leaving the chalice suspended in the air, the angel knelt down beside the children and repeated three times: "Most

Holy Trinity, Father, Son and Holy Spirit, I offer you the most precious body, blood, soul and divinity of Jesus Christ, present in all the tabernacles of the world, in reparation for the outrages, sacrileges and indifference with which He himself is offended. And, through the infinite merits of His most Sacred Heart and the Immaculate Heart of Mary, I beg of you the conversion of poor sinners."[6] Rising the angel gave the host to Lucia and shared the blood from the chalice with Jacinta and Francisco. He said, "Take and drink the body and blood of Jesus Christ horribly outraged by ungrateful men! Make reparation for their crimes and console your God."[7] Once again the angel prostrated himself on the ground and repeated the same prayer; he then disappeared.

Such were the apparitions which preceded Mary's message at Fatima. Quite certainly the children were in awe at what had transpired. Yet, they were much bewildered and wondered what all of this meant. Answers to the questions were not long in coming as in May 1917 the world began to hear the message of the need and value of the rosary.

Apparitions of Our Lady of the Rosary

On Sunday May 13, 1917 the apparitions of our Blessed Mother at Fatima began. Following Mass Lucia, Jacinta and Francisco were playing near the Cova da Iria while the sheep they were tending grazed on the nearby countryside. A flash of light pierced the air, frightening the children. Although they saw no clouds the children rounded up the sheep, thinking that a storm was imminent. Suddenly another shaft of light split the sky. As they fled in fear the children came upon a beautiful lady standing over the foliage of a small holmoak tree. Lucia records the scene: "It was a lady dressed in white, more brilliant than the sun, shedding rays of light, clear and stronger than a crystal glass filled with the most sparkling water, pierced by the burning rays of the sun."[8] The woman told the children not to be afraid. Lucia asked the lady her origin. "I am from heaven," came the reply. "I have come to ask you to come here for six consecutive months on the thirteenth day at this same hour. I will tell you later who I am and what I want."[9] The woman promised to take the children to heaven while warning them that they would suffer much in reparation for the sins by which God was offended. The lady spoke again: "Say the rosary every day to earn peace for the world and the end of the war."[10] After this the lady elevated herself and traveled east until she disappeared from sight.

The vision placed the children in a state of awe while lending insight into the purpose of their previous encounters with the Angel of Peace. During the apparition only Lucia was able to see and communicate with the lady. Jacinta was able to see and hear her. Francisco saw her only after prayer; he never heard her speak.[11]

As with the apparitions of the Angel of Peace the children agreed to keep the vision a secret. Jacinta, however, was too full of life for a child of eight to keep quiet. The Marto family did not initially believe Jacinta's story, and they were amused at her comments. It did not take long for Lucia's parents to hear the story. They accused Lucia of lying and threatened to lock her in her room. The children continued to tend the sheep during the ensuing days of May and early June. They would give their lunches to the sheep or needy children as an act of sacrifice. They now understood the meaning of our Lady's words that they would suffer much by making reparation for sins.

June 13, 1917 seemed like an eternity in coming for the children. The Feast of St. Anthony was a special celebration for the local community. It was hoped by the Santos and Marto families that the children would go to the festivities in the village rather than return to the Cova da Iria. News of the children's vision had spread to several surrounding districts and people came to see the children as the time for our Lady's appearance neared.

The children went to the Cova da Iria as instructed by the woman from heaven. Although many others were present, the Lady came as before with a flash of light and stood upon the holmoak. She told the children, "Say the rosary, inserting between the mysteries the following prayer — O my Jesus forgive us. Save us from the fires of Hell. Lead all souls to Heaven, especially those in most need." The woman continued, "Jesus wants to establish devotion to my Immaculate Heart in the world. I will never leave you: my Immaculate Heart will be your refuge and the way that will lead you to God."[12] During the second apparition the Lady told the children a secret not to be revealed. Although many tried to extract the secret, the children held firm and told nothing.

As a result of the second apparition the children continued to be persecuted, questioned and punished by family members and friends alike. Doubt reigned supreme in the local community. There were believers but they were few and scattered. People from the surrounding areas, however, were very profoundly struck by the whole combination of events. Word spread rapidly and many people began to plan for July 13th, the next promised date for the appearance of the woman from Heaven.

The period between the second and third apparition was a very troublesome time for Lucia. As the eldest of the group (she was only ten) she was questioned very severely by both her parents and officials. Through the influence of the local parish priest and her parents, Lucia became convinced that the whole affair was the work of the devil. She decided, therefore, not to go to the Cova da Iria in July. She informed Jacinta and Francisco of her decision.

On July 13 for some unknown reason Lucia's doubt about the apparitions left her. She went at the appointed hour to her cousins' home. They were crying, assuming that Lucia was not going to the Cova. On seeing her, however, Jacinta and Francisco jumped to their feet and walked joyfully to the Cova for their appointment with the Lady from Heaven. The crowds along the way were thick, as many people from the surrounding regions had come in hopes that the children could ask the Lady's intercession for sick family members and friends.

When the children arrived at the Cova they began to pray the rosary as they had previously done. As before, the Lady began to come from the East; soon she rested above the holmoak. She told the children, "Continue to say the rosary everyday in honor of Our Lady of the Rosary to obtain peace for the world and the end of the war, for she alone can save it."[13] Lucia asked the Lady to identify herself and to perform a miracle so all would believe. The Lady answered, "Continue to come here every month. In October I will say who I am and what I desire and I will perform a miracle all shall see so that they will believe."[14]

After telling the children they would need to sacrifice themselves for sinners, an amazing vision was beheld. The light reflecting from the Lady's hands seemed to penetrate the earth and the children saw a sea of fire with devils and souls in human form floating in the fire. The children were terrified and raised their eyes to the Lady. She explained,

> "You have seen Hell, where the souls of poor sinners go. To save them God wants to establish throughout the world devotion to my Immaculate Heart. If people will do what I tell you, many souls will be saved, and there will be peace. The war is going to end. But, if people do not stop offending God, another and worse war will break out in the reign of Pius XI. When you see a night illumined by an unknown light, know that it is a sign that God gives you, that He is going to punish the world for its crimes by means of war, hunger, persecution of the Church and of the Holy Father. To forestall this, I shall come to ask the consecration of Russia to my Immaculate Heart and the Communion of Reparation on the First Saturdays. If they heed my request, Russia will be converted, and there will be peace. If not, she shall spread her errors throughout the world, promoting wars and persecutions of the Church; the good will be martyred, the Holy Father will have much to suffer, [and] various nations will be annihilated. In the end, my Immaculate Heart shall triumph. The Holy Father will consecrate Russia to me, which will be converted, and some time of peace will be given to the world."

The Lady concluded, "Do not tell this message to anyone except Francisco."[15]

Lucia wanted to do something for the Lady after having been entrusted with such information. "Don't you want anything else from me," she cried. "No," the Lady responded, "today I desire nothing else from you."[16] With that the Lady from Heaven again elevated herself above the holmoak and drifted off to the East.

Following the third apparition of the woman, troubles for the children, especially Lucia, began to mount drastically. On August

11 the three children and their parents were summoned to the local magistrate's office to answer many accusations which had been registered about the recent happenings at the Cova da Iria. Lucia's parents went but Lucia was allowed to speak for herself. Ti and Olimpia Marto would not allow their children to go; Senor Marto answered the summons himself. The meeting was short. The magistrate tried to extract the secret message of the third apparition from Lucia, but failed on all accounts. Senor Santos claimed that the whole affair was a hoax and told the magistrate he did not believe. Ti Marto, however, fully supported his children and their elder cousin and stated that he and his wife were believers.

On August 13, the date for the next apparition, the magistrate came to Aljustrel and the home of Jacinta and Francisco Marto. After a few questions, the magistrate managed to lure the three children (Lucia was visiting) into his carriage, convincing them that he could take them to the Cova da Iria faster. Instead of heading for the Cova, the carriage sped off to the magistrate's home, nine miles from Fatima; the children had been taken prisoner. For two days the children were held in jail and interrogated by the magistrate. In trying to extract the secret the magistrate threatened the children with death from burning oil. Nevertheless, the children held fast through prayer and offering their sufferings to the Immaculate Heart of Mary for the reparation of sins as they had been instructed. Finally, on August 15, the children were released to the local parish priest in Fatima. As soon as the children returned home they proceeded to the Cova da Iria for prayer.

On Sunday, August 19, Lucia, Francisco, and Francisco's elder brother John left Aljustrel for Valinhos, a neighboring village, to spend the afternoon. At about four o'clock Lucia began to notice the signs which preceded the apparitions of our Lady. She told John to hasten and bring Jacinta, giving him four pennies for his efforts. John hesitated, wanting to see the Lady himself. He eventually left, however, and found Jacinta at her godmother's home. As Jacinta arrived on the scene the Lady appeared to them over a holmoak a little higher than the one at the Cova da Iria. "What do you want of me?" Lucia asked. "I want you to continue to come to Cova da Iria on the 13th and to continue to say the rosary every day."[17] Lucia told the Lady of her anguish at the inability of many to believe in her real presence. She asked the Lady if she would be willing to perform a miracle that all might see and believe. "Yes," the Lady answered, "In the last month, in October, I shall perform a miracle so that all may believe in my apparitions. If they had not taken you to the village, the miracle would have been greater."[18]

Lucia asked the Lady what should be done with money which had been given for the relief of loved ones. The Lady told her, "Use half of the money received for litters [for the poor]. . . . The other half should be set aside to help build a chapel on this spot." The Lady then said, "Pray! Pray a great deal and make sacrifices for sinners, for many souls go to Hell for not having someone to pray and make sacrifices for them."[19] After these words the Lady again drifted toward the heavens in the East.

The children took a branch from the holmoak at Valinhos to show their parents. The branch had a very fragrant yet indescribable fragrance. It was noticed by all, including Maria Rosa Santos, Lucia's mother. From this time on, Lucia's parents began to change in their attitude toward the apparitions. Their change of heart had come from something they could not explain.

Between the fourth and fifth apparitions Lucia, Francisco and Jacinta began to practice more severe forms of mortification and suffering for the reparation of sins. The children, for example, would not drink water during the day while they tended the sheep. They continued to give their lunches to more needy children they would encounter each day. At times the children would tie a coarse rope around their waists and keep it there all day and night despite its uncomfortable nature.

When September 13 dawned the community of Fatima was crowded with people, some who had come from great distances. The Santos and Marto homes were inundated with people who had requests to place before the Lady from Heaven. The crowds were so thick along the route to the Cova da Iria that the children had trouble making the trip by the appointed hour.

Upon arrival at the Cova the children began to pray the rosary in anticipation of the Lady's arrival. As the children were praying the fifth decade of the rosary the Lady came to them over the holmoak, preceded by a flash of light as in all previous appearances. The Lady said, "Let the people continue to pray the rosary every day to obtain the end of the war." The Lady then reiterated her promise of August, telling the children that a miracle would occur for all to believe. She said, "In October I shall perform a miracle so that all may believe in my apparitions. . . . Saint Joseph will come with Baby Jesus to give peace to the world. Our Lord will come to bless the people. Our Lady of Sorrows and our Lady of Mount Carmel will also come. Additionally, the Lady said, "God is pleased with your sacrifices but does not wish that you sleep with the rope. Wear it only during the day."[20] Following this conversation the Lady departed toward the East.

After the September 13 apparition a great dichotomy of opinion sprang up concerning the visions. The official Church position was skeptical at best. The parish priest in Fatima continued to discredit the children on all fronts. Although his opposition to the whole affair was well-known throughout the community and surrounding countryside, the local people were equally as strident about their support. Many thought that with a promised miracle less than thirty days away the great proof would be forthcoming. The continual support of Ti and Olimpia Marto, along with the now strong support of the Santos family, gave the children the courage to see the affair through. The pressure on Lucia, Francisco and Jacinta was great; their parents' support kept them going.

October 13, 1917, the date of the promised miracle, dawned cool and rainy. The weather did not dampen the spirits of the thousands of people who had come from all over Portugal to witness the promised miracle. Reporters from daily newspapers had been sent to cover the story. The crowd at the Cova was estimated at seventy to one hundred thousand, despite the miserable weather conditions.[21]

Because of the massive crowd and in fear of their safety, the children were escorted to the Cova da Iria by their parents. As noon approached the children were in their normal place. "Silence, silence, the Lady is coming," cried Lucia as she saw the familiar flash of light. The rain cleared almost on command and the sun began to gradually appear. The Lady rested on the holmoak as before. The Lady told Lucia, "I want to tell you that they must build a chapel here in my honor, that I am the Lady of the Rosary and that people must continue to pray the rosary everyday. The war will end and the soldiers will return to their homes soon." Lucia asked if the favors she had previously requested would be granted. The Lady replied, "Some I will, others I will not! People must mend their lives and ask forgiveness for their sins. Offend not our Lord anymore, for He is already much offended." The Lady concluded, "I desire nothing else from you."[22]

As the Lady began her ascent to heaven the children beheld a spectacular vision. The sun, though formerly bright, became pale as the moon. To the left of the sun, St. Joseph appeared, holding in his left arm the child Jesus. St. Joseph emerged from the bright clouds only to his chest, sufficient to allow him to raise his right hand and make, together with the child Jesus, the sign of the cross three times over the world. As St. Joseph and the child Jesus blessed the world, our Lady stood in all her brilliancy to the right of the sun, dressed in the blue and white robes of our Lady of the Rosary.

Meanwhile, Francisco and Jacinta were bathed in the marvelous colors and signs of the sun. Lucia was privileged to see our Lord dressed in red as the Divine Redeemer, blessing the world. Beside him stood our Lady, dressed now in the purple robes of our Lady of Sorrows. Finally, the Blessed Virgin appeared again to Lucia in all her ethereal brightness, clothed in the simple brown robes of Mount Carmel.

As the children stared enraptured by these most beautiful heavenly visions, the countless thousands of people were amazed and overpowered by other miracles in the sky. The sun had taken on an extraordinary color. Ti Marto later testified, "We could look at the sun with ease, it did not bother us at all. It seemed to be continually fading and glowing in one fashion, then another. It threw shafts of light one way and another painting everything in different colors, the people, trees, earth and even the air."[23] The promised miracle had begun, but there was much more to behold. Ti Marto continued, "Everybody stood still and quiet, gazing at the sun. At a certain point the sun stopped its play of light and then started dancing. It stopped once, then again began to dance until it seemed to loosen itself from the skies and fall upon the people. It was a moment of terrible suspense. At last the sun reversed its path, returning to its proper rest in the sky."[24]

O Seculo, a Lisbon daily newspaper, carried a detailed account of the extraordinary event:

> From the height of the road where the people parked their carriages and where many hundreds stood, afraid to brave the muddy soil, we saw the immense multitude turn towards the sun at its highest, free of all clouds. The sun called to mind a plate of dull silver. It could be stared at without the least effort. It did not burn or blind. It seemed that an eclipse was taking place. All of a sudden a tremendous shout burst forth [from the people], "Miracle, miracle! Marvel, marvel." Before the astonished eyes of the people, the sun trembled and made some brusque unnatural movements, beyond all cosmic laws; the sun danced in the typical expression of the peasants.[25]

A fitting ending to the miracle of the sun was in order. The thousands of pilgrims in the area noticed that upon the sun's return to its proper place in the sky that all their clothes were completely dry despite the heavy rain that had poured down earlier. Additionally, the ground was dry. Truly, the Lady from Heaven had made good her promise to create a miracle so that all would believe.

The Aftermath of the Visions

Following the miracle of October 13 no doubt remained in the mind of anyone. It was difficult for the children and their families to return to their routine lives in the Portuguese countryside. People continued for many months to hound the families asking the children to intercede for them to the Virgin Mary for requests of all sorts. It was not long after the visions, however, that it became plain that Francisco and Jacinta would soon depart this life and enter their final home as promised by our Lady.

Francisco had been told by the Lady he would go to heaven but first he would have to pray many rosaries.[26] He never forgot these words and became a true disciple of the prayer. He seemed to have no other interest in life. People came to question him about what he wanted to do as an adult. He would always say, "I don't want to be anything. I just want to die and go to heaven."[27] Knowing that his death was not far off, Francisco gave himself more and more to self-mortification and prayer.

In October 1918, only one year after the miracle, Francisco contracted a severe case of influenza. Although very sick he kept his selfsame spirit of love and sacrifice. Though he knew it was hopeless, Francisco took all the medicines which the doctors had prescribed, pleasing his parents in the hopes for his recovery.

By December Francisco had recovered sufficiently to take short walks. He always went to the Cova da Iria to pray. His principal desire was to console our Lord and our Lady who seemed so sorrowful from the sins of all people. Jacinta and Lucia would visit Francisco which gave him renewed strength. Francisco desired to receive his first communion before he died. This was arranged and he received our Lord witnessed by Jacinta and Lucia.

Shortly thereafter, Francisco began to fail rapidly. His pain was great but he never complained. Rather, he offered his suffering for the reparation of sins and to the Immaculate Heart of Mary. His mother watched over him. Though her constant prayer was that "God's will be done," it did not lessen the sorrow of her heart as she watched Francisco die before her eyes. On Friday morning, April 4, 1919, our Lord came to claim Francisco as his own. The next day he was buried in the local cemetery. Lucia attended but Jacinta, too sick herself, stayed home in bed.

The influenza epidemic which hit the Marto home affected Jacinta as well as Francisco. Her condition grew much worse after Francisco's death as an abscess formed on her chest. Olimpia Marto, after losing Francisco, felt that much more sadness for her little girl. Jacinta would tell her, "Don't worry, Mother, for I'm going to heaven. I'll pray a lot for you there."[28]

Early in June of 1919 a doctor came to the Marto home and advised that Jacinta be taken to the hospital at Orem for better treatment. Jacinta knew the doctors would not be able to cure her but she went willingly in obedience to her parents thinking it would provide her a greater opportunity to sacrifice herself. The hardest thing for Jacinta would be to leave her family and especially Lucia. Jacinta stayed at Orem for two months. Her only visitors during that period were her mother and Lucia, who came once for a two-day visit. The doctors agreed in late August that she was making no progress in the hospital so they discharged her to be with her family.

Jacinta continued during her illness to offer sacrifice for the reparation of sins. Although very difficult she took without complaint all medicines, soups and food that her mother gave her. Additionally, she would continue to say the Angel's prayer, sneaking from the bed so as to bow fully as the three children had been taught. Despite her condition Jacinta continually gave encouragement to Lucia for the mission ahead:

> Soon I shall go to heaven. You are to stay here to reveal that the Lord wants to establish throughout the world devotion to the Immaculate Heart of Mary. Tell everyone that Our Lord grants us all graces through the Immaculate Heart of Mary, that all must make their petitions to her and that the Sacred Heart of Jesus desires that the Immaculate Heart of Mary be venerated at the same time. Tell them that they should all ask for peace from the Immaculate Heart of Mary, as God has placed it in her hands. Oh, if I could only put in the heart of everyone in the world the fire that is burning in me and makes me love so much the Heart of Jesus and the Heart of Mary.[29]

During her illness, our Lady appeared to Jacinta informing her that she soon would go to a hospital in Lisbon. As Jacinta announced the revelation everyone thought her to be dreaming but only a few days later a specialist in children's diseases from Lisbon called at the Marto home. It was decided to send Jacinta to Lisbon under the doctor's care. Before leaving, Jacinta begged her parents to take her to the Cova da Iria one last time. The request was granted. The following day Jacinta said goodbye to her beloved Lucia; their parting was a bitter cross to bear. Lucia recounted Jacinta's final words to her: "Never again shall we see each other. Pray a great deal for me for I am going to Heaven. There I will pray a lot for you. Love Jesus a great deal and the Immaculate Heart of Mary. Make many sacrifices for sinners."[30]

At the hospital Jacinta was diagnosed as having purulent pleurisy. It was decided that surgery was the best possible solution to the problem. Because of her condition a general anesthetic was not used; the local anesthesia did a poor job of killing the pain. The doctors removed two ribs and appeared hopeful for success. Jacinta warned them, "It is all in vain. Our Lady told me that I am going to die soon."[31] On February 20, 1920, Jacinta asked for the last rites (today the Sacrament of the Sick) of the Church. A priest was called who heard her confession and anointed her. She asked to receive communion but the priest said he would be back the next morning with Viaticum. Jacinta died peacefully that evening without having her wish fulfilled.

Lucia dos Santos, the sole surviving seer of Fatima, began her mission, the one Jacinta had mentioned, four years after the apparitions. On June 17, 1921, Lucia departed for a convent school run by the Sisters of St. Dorothy. She was instructed by the local bishop to say nothing of the Fatima apparitions. At the school she registered as Maria dos Dores to conceal her true identity. Her religious name in the community was Sister Maria of the Sorrows.

On December 10, 1925, while at the convent, our Lady again appeared to Lucia. The child Jesus was at our Lady's side, elevated upon a cloud of light. Our Lady, resting one hand upon Lucia's shoulder, held in her other hand a heart surrounded with thorns. The child Jesus spoke first to Lucia: "Have pity on the Heart of your most Holy Mother. It is covered with the thorns with which ungrateful men pierce it at every movement, and there is no one to remove them with an act of reparation."[32]

Then our Lady said to Lucia, "My daughter, look at my Heart encircled with the thorns with which ungrateful men pierce it at every movement by their blasphemies and ingratitude. Announce in my name that I promise to assist at the hour of death with the graces necessary for salvation all those who, on the first Saturday of five consecutive months, go to confession and receive Holy Communion, recite the rosary and keep me company for a quarter of an hour while meditating on the mysteries of the rosary with the intention of making reparation to me."[33]

Lucia revealed the vision to her confessor and the Mother Superior of her community. A year passed and on December 15, 1926 the child Jesus again appeared to Lucia, inquiring if she had spread the devotion of reparation to the Immaculate Heart of Mary. Lucia responded that her confessor had described the pitfalls of such a devotion while her Mother Superior had thought the devotion a good idea. In her cloistered position, Lucia had not been able to effectively plant the seeds for devotion to the Immaculate Heart of Mary. In 1927, Lucia was transferred to a convent at Tuy, Spain. One day that year, while praying in the convent chapel, Lucia was given permission from heaven to reveal the two parts of the secret revealed to the children in July 1917, the vision of Hell and the need for devotion to the Immaculate Heart of Mary. She informed her confessor, the Mother Superior and the Bishop of Leiria (the diocese of Fatima). Two years later, in 1929, our Lady again appeared to Lucia at Tuy. She made the following request: "I have come to ask the consecration of Russia to my Immaculate Heart. . . . If they heed my request, Russia will be converted and there will be peace."[34] Our Lady explained that this consecration should be made by the Holy Father in unison with all the bishops of the world. The request went to the local bishop who brought this request to the attention of the Holy Father. Three years passed with no action. Again Lucia wrote to the bishop: nothing happened.

In 1940 Lucia again wrote the Bishop of Leiria expressing her regret that the consecration had not yet been made. Then, at the command of her spiritual director Lucia wrote directly to Pope Pius XII. Lucia asked for the consecration of the world to Mary's Immaculate Heart with a special mention of Russia. Finally on October 31, 1942 the bishops of Portugal gathered at the Cathedral of Lisbon to join the Holy Father in fulfilling the request of our

Lady. Pope Pius XII consecrated the Church and the world to Mary's Immaculate Heart including the people of Russia by the words: "Give peace to peoples separated from us by error or by schism and especially to those who profess such singular devotion to thee and in whose homes an honored place was ever accorded thy venerable image (today perhaps often hidden to await better days); bring them back to the one fold of Christ under the one true Shepherd."[35] Six weeks later, on the Feast of the Immaculate Conception, in the presence of 40,000 people, the pope repeated the consecration at St. Peter's in Rome.

In 1948 Lucia became a member of a cloistered community of Carmelite nuns in Coimbra, Portugal. Her name is now Sister Mary of the Immaculate Heart.

Summary

The story and message of Fatima is clear: pray the rosary everyday for the reparation of sins. In coming to Fatima with a message of prayer and peace, the Blessed Virgin Mary has herself given to the world the true value of the rosary. Although somewhat eclipsed in its present devotion, the rosary, as evidenced by the powerful message of Fatima, will continue to be a powerful tool in the ever present battle to maintain peace in our very difficult and complex world.

Following the presage of the Angel of Peace in 1916, three peasant children, Lucia dos Santos and Francisco and Jacinta Marto, were privileged to be seers of the Blessed Virgin Mary. Although their story was challenged they continued to go to the Cova da Iria to meet with the beautiful woman from heaven and hear her message. Even imprisonment from local officials could not counter the courage of the three children pitted against a world not ready for the message they were commissioned to deliver.

Only after the miracle of the sun on October 13, 1917 was the world able to believe. It became the task of Lucia, the eldest of the three, to deliver Mary's message to the world. Within two years of the apparitions both Francisco and Jacinta had died, called by

God at an early age to enjoy everlasting happiness in heaven. Lucia, joining the Sisters of St. Dorothy, continued to receive visions and instructions from Mary and the child Jesus. Through much perseverance she was able to convince her superiors that the consecration of the world, especially Russia, to Mary's Immaculate Heart was the solution designated by God to promote world peace. On October 31, 1942, Pope Pius XII gathered together the bishops of Portugal and consecrated the world to Mary. Although there is much debate today as to whether the consecration was accomplished according to Mary's specific instructions, our Lady's appearances at Fatima have greatly encouraged devotion to the rosary.

Today a beautiful basilica and massive courtyard stand in the Cova da Iria, a tribute to the events which took place there. For pilgrims today Fatima continues to be a place where the message of Mary is lived out on a daily basis. The promises of Mary were great but the price seems to be high. One visit to Fatima, however, will prove to the most skeptical person that the cost of peace is worth the effort.

Chapter 8 — Notes

1. In 1858 the Virgin Mary was seen by Bernadette Soubirous in a series of apparitions. Today Lourdes is the most popular Marian shrine and is visited by millions each year, many of whom are seeking a physical cure to various ailments. Since the apparitions, there have been many medically unexplainable cures provided at Lourdes.
2. Lucia dos Santos (Sr. Mary of the Immaculate Heart), *Lucia Speaks — Memoirs and Letters of the Last-Surviving Seer of Fatima*, trans. Dominican Nuns of the Perpetual Rosary (Washington, NJ: AMI Press, 1976), p. 72.
3. *Ibid.*
4. *Ibid.*
5. *Ibid.*, p. 74.
6. *Ibid.*, p. 75.
7. *Ibid.*
8. *Ibid.*, p. 194.
9. *Ibid.*, p. 195.
10. *Ibid.*, p. 197.
11. See William Thomas Walsh, *Our Lady of Fatima* (Garden City, NY: Image Books, 1954), pp. 65-73. Additionally, in her memoirs, *Lucia Speaks*, Lucia dos Santos mentions that Francisco was not privileged to hear Mary's voice.

12. Dos Santos, *Lucia Speaks*, p. 198.
13. *Ibid.*, p. 199.
14. *Ibid.*
15. *Ibid.*, p. 200.
16. *Ibid.*, p. 201.
17. *Ibid.*
18. John De Marchi, I.M.C., *Mother of Christ Crusade* Billings, MT: Mother of Christ Crusade, 1947), ch. 7, p. 21.
19. Dos Santos, *Lucia Speaks*, p. 202.
20. De Marchi, *Crusade*, ch. 8, p. 8.
21. See Walsh, *Our Lady of Fatima*, pp. 137-40, and De Marchi, *Crusade*, especially pp. 1-9.
22. Dos Santos, *Lucia Speaks*, p. 206.
23. De Marchi, *Crusade*, ch. 10, p. 4.
24. *Ibid.*, pp. 4-5.
25. *Ibid.*, pp. 7-8.
26. This fact was revealed to Francisco during the first apparition on May 13, 1917.
27. De Marchi, *Crusade*, ch. 11, p. 5.
28. *Ibid.*, ch. 12, p. 1.
29. *Ibid.*, p. 7.
30. *Ibid.*, p. 11.
31. *Ibid.*, p. 19.
32. *Ibid.*, ch. 14, p. 9.
33. *Ibid.*, p. 11.
34. *Ibid.*, p. 17.
35. See *Queen of Apostles Prayerbook* (St. Paul Edition, 1972), p. 179.
36. De Marchi, *Crusade*, ch. 14, p. 23.

Chapter 9
The Story of the Rosary —
A Summary

The story of the rosary is rich with tradition, devotion and historical fact. In this book the origins of this most efficacious of prayer devotions to the Virgin Mary have been discussed. Additionally, many facets of culture which have been influenced by the rosary, but do not neatly fit into the historical derivation of the prayer, have been outlined. One thing is certain: the rosary has been a major influence in Roman Catholic thought for over 500 years while paving the way for a greater understanding of the mystery of Christ celebrated within family prayer.

This effort began by investigating various theories as to how the rosary that we know today came into existence. Through the tradition the story of St. Dominic and the rosary had become an accepted belief. It can be shown historically, however, that this story is apocryphal. Two hundred years after St. Dominic's death, Blessed Alanus de Rupe, a Dominican monk, published the legendary account of Dominic's encounter with the Virgin. Although Dominican influence in the promotion of the rosary had been strong, there is no indication that Dominic was personally invested with the rosary or instructions for its use by the Virgin Mary. In this book I have opted for an evolutionary progression of rosary development. This progression somewhat chronologically parallels the development of prayer beads in Islam, although cross-influences between these developments is hard to trace.

The historical development of the rosary begins with the Desert Fathers and their need to find a system to ease their laborious and repetitive prayer life. Prayer counters such as rocks, sticks or notches in wood were effectively employed by these anchorites to assure that the proper number of prayers were recited. Over time and contingent with the development of the monastic lifestyle, counters and psalms were united into a *Na tri coicat* format so that "fifties" could be used for personal and/or penitential prayer.

As the need for lay participation in the prayer life of the Church increased, the need for a Psalter of popular prayers (most people of the period were not sufficiently educated to pray the psalms in Latin) became urgent. Thus the *Na tri coicat* format was imposed first on recitations of *Paternosters* and later on *Aves*. Spurred by the association of Mary with roses and rose gardens, from both scriptural and traditional bases, the Marian Psalter of *Aves* became by the fourteenth century a standard form of repetitive prayer for the whole Church, laity and religious alike.

The fifteenth century saw the rosary begin its development into the familiar prayer form we know today. During this period the formation of the individual prayers, plus the development of the mysteries took place. The Our Father came intact from the Gospel of Matthew. The development of the other prayers is evolutionary as is the rosary as a whole. The Hail Mary developed from the scriptural greetings of Gabriel and Elizabeth to Mary in Luke's Gospel, plus a popular exhortation in use by the laity of that period. Although forms of the prayer were in use for some 300 years previous, it is only with the Council of Trent in the sixteenth century that the Hail Mary achieved the form so popular today. The Glory Be was used as a common doxology from the earliest of Christian times when praying the psalms. The Apostles' Creed and *Salve Regina* are later additions to the rosary format. Although the origins can be traced to late medieval times their addition to the rosary is not found until the late sixteenth to early seventeenth centuries.

The mysteries, the true essence of the rosary, have their origin from the genius of Henry of Kalbar who appended clausulae to each of the fifty *Aves* of the Marian Psalter. The development of the mysteries included first the fixing of 150 clausulae which were followed by the introduction of fifteen true mysteries, one for each *Paternoster*. Eventually the clausulae faded away and the fifteen mysteries remained. By the mid-sixteenth century the mysteries we know today, divided into sorrowful, joyful and glorious, were in place and used in rosary recitation.

The sixteenth century is the most important for the historical derivation of the rosary for it was in this century that this prayer was officially recognized by the Roman Catholic Church. The single most significant event in the Church's recognition of the rosary was the formation in 1470 of the Confraternity of the Rosary by Blessed Alanus de Rupe. This organization was very popular, gathering some 500,000 members by 1479. With the requirements for membership being minimal the growing membership of the Confraternity raised the consciousness of the people to the efficacy of the rosary. Furthering the popularity of the rosary was the publishing in the early sixteenth century of a series of popular rosary books, including the work of Alberto da Castello.

The Confraternity's work was finalized in 1571 with recognition by Rome of the rosary. Pope St. Pius V on October 7, 1571 declared that because of the efficacious assistance of the rosary in securing victory over the Turks at Lepanto a commemoration in honor of the rosary would henceforth be held on that date. Two years later the Feast of the Most Holy Rosary was established by Pope Gregory XIII; the date is still celebrated in the contemporary liturgical calendar.

The seventeenth century was highlighted by the work of St. Louis de Montfort and his book *The Wonderful Secret of the Rosary*. This book was notable for its integration of history and devotion to the rosary. Additionally, pastoral application of the prayer for all peoples was a strong emphasis of the book. The work of St. Louis de Montfort projected the rosary into the twentieth century.

On the eve of this century the rosary found its greatest papal advocate, Pope Leo XIII. Pope Leo during his twenty-five year pontificate wrote twelve encyclical letters plus many additional exhortations, letters and constitutions that dealt with the rosary. Several important concepts concerning the rosary were born from the pen of Pope Leo. It was Leo who continued to reiterate the importance of rosary promotion, especially during the month of October. More importantly, Pope Leo in *Fidentem piumque* stressed that the rosary could be efficacious in unlocking the chief mysteries of the faith. The pope was also a great advocate of the rosary as a cure for the ills of society, both secularly in day-to-day life and spiritually as a tool to further the cause of ecumenism. Finally, Pope Leo reestablished the Confraternity of the Rosary under the guidance of the Dominican order. There is no question that as the twentieth century dawned, the rosary had found its most loyal and vocal friend in Pope Leo XIII.

In our own century the voices of those who have promoted the rosary have continued to speak. All of the pontiffs of this century (with the exception of the one-month pontificate of Pope John Paul I) have written on the efficacious nature of the rosary. Probably the most significant comment which has come forward is the emphasis on the family as the principal body around which the rosary can be most effectively utilized. Along with the encyclical *Ingruentium malorum* of Pope Pius XII, this cause has been championed by Father Patrick Peyton, the Rosary Priest. Father Peyton's crusade for family prayer and the rosary can be summarized by his famous saying, "The family that prays together, stays together."

Popes John XXIII and Paul VI emphasized the importance of the mysteries in rosary devotion. Pope John gave the mysteries a three-fold purpose: mystical contemplation, intimate reflection and pious intention. Pope Paul considered the rosary a hollow shell without the mysteries. The views of the pontiffs show that rosary recitation and teaching continues to be important in our contemporary prayer devotion.

Throughout the historical development of the rosary this prayer and its symbolic manifestations in beads and roses has been present in artistic expression. Before the fifteenth century the main theme in art expressive of the rosary was the image of the rose garden and its association with the Marian Psalter. Many paintings of the period showed roses and rose gardens in scenes depicting the Virgin Mary. Through the mastery of such artists as Stefano da Zevio, roses and the Psalter became forever joined. The Madonna of the Rose Garden was a second important theme of pre-Renaissance art. This concept became popular in works by Stephan Lochner and Antonello da Messina which foreshadowed the famous Madonna and Child motif of the Renaissance period.

By the dawn of the sixteenth century the beads themselves became the main focus of rosary art. Works abound which show the beads as necklaces, prayer counters or even play toys for the child Jesus. Additionally, the beads were shown in many scenes with saints. St. Dominic was a popular subject, even though the rosary as such did not exist as depicted in the saint's lifetime. The Madonna and Child with the beads predominantly displayed was the primary scene depicted during the period. The Renaissance saw the use of a particular color scheme which delineated the various mysteries, white for joyful, red for sorrowful and yellow or gold for the glorious.

Although painting was the predominant art form which expressed the theme of rosary devotion, sculpture and the altarpiece also presented this theme. Statues of the Virgin or Madonna and Child began to appear with the rosary beads in use. Altarpieces in Germany depicted decades of rosary beads while various panels in the altar depicted the fifteen mysteries.

The story we have described is the history of the rosary as developed within the Christian consciousness. Christianity, however, was probably the last great world religion to use a prayer counter in its daily worship. Of the great world religions, Hinduism, Buddhism and Islam were all using their own forms of rosaries before Christianity.

It is generally agreed by scholars that a system for counting repetitive prayers began with the Hindus some nine centuries before Christ. In Brahminical writings of the ninth century B.C.E. we find the first clear indications of a Hindu rosary. Over many centuries two different forms of Hindu rosaries evolved, based primarily on the worship of the two gods Siva and Visnu. Today followers of Siva use a prayer counter of thirty-two or sixty-four beads; those who follow Visnu use a rosary of 108 beads. Both groups use the counters for mental prayer in the repetitive recitation of the many characteristics of greatness which each god possesses.

In Buddhism one finds the widest use and diffusion of the rosary. Influenced greatly by the Hindus, Buddhists principally use a rosary of 108 beads upon which are remembered the important mysteries of the faith. In Buddhism, rosary practice is very much affected by sect, position and ritual significance. The many permutations that can be created through these three concepts make rosary use and practice extremely varied and multifaceted. Buddhist practices in Korea and Japan show the two ends of the spectrum. In Korea a counter of 110 beads, each with its own name, is used. Reciting the proper prayer at the proper time of day will bring prosperity to the land. In Japan the rosary used is very complex. A full recitation of the beads will require the saying of over 36,000 prayers.

The use of prayer beads in Islam was developed along parallel but different lines to that of Christianity. In the ninth century of the Christian era, approximately 200 years after the death of the prophet Muhammad, Muslims began to use prayer beads in their daily rhythm of prayer. Islam uses a rosary of ninety-nine beads, upon which are recited the names and attributes of Allah. The Muslim rosary beads are also used in repetitive incantations which are common practice in the five-fold daily prayer routine of the faith.

The story of the Christian rosary cannot end without an analysis of the visions at Fatima and Mary's powerful message to pray the rosary daily. From May to October 1917 three peasant children, Lucia dos Santos and her cousins Francisco and Jacinta Marto, were privileged to be seers of the visions of Fatima. Although the children were harassed and even imprisoned by the local magistrate, their faith and diligence in meeting with the Lady of the Rosary proved a great triumph for the rosary and its promotion throughout the world. Through the visions of October 13, 1917, including the miracle of the sun witnessed by thousands on the scene, the world came to know that the apparitions of Fatima were real. It was evident with the rosary that the world had a weapon which if properly utilized could bring peace to our troubled society.

Our story is thus complete. We have traced the rosary and its predecessors from the ninth century B.C.E. to the words of the National Conference of Catholic Bishops in 1983. Although our primary focus has been on the development of the Christian rosary, we have seen that other great religions also use counters in their daily prayers. Armed with the rosary Christians today have a powerful tool to call upon God's assistance through the intercession of the Virgin Mary. The tradition and tools are present; the response of the faithful today is awaited.

Appendix:
Indulgences Granted to the Rosary

Since papal approval of the Confraternity of the Rosary in 1475, many indulgences have been granted by Rome for Confraternity members. Additionally, the faithful at large have been granted numerous indulgences for rosary recitation. The indulgences contained herein were effective until January 1, 1967. At that time Pope Paul VI issued a new *Enchiridion of Indulgences* which revoked all former indulgences except those contained in the new *Enchiridion*. Article 48 of this document gives the presently accepted indulgences for rosary use.

Recitation of the Marian Rosary
(*Rosarii marialis recitatio*)

A *plenary indulgence* is granted, if the Rosary is recited in a church or public oratory or in a family group, a religious Community or pious Association; a *partial indulgence* is granted in other circumstances.

"Now the Rosary is a certain formula of prayer, which is made up of fifteen decades of 'Hail Marys' with an 'Our Father' before each decade, and in which the recitation of each decade is accompanied by pious meditation on a particular mystery of our Redemption." (*Roman Breviary*)

The name "Rosary," however, is commonly used in reference to only a third part of the fifteen decades.

The gaining of the *plenary indulgence* is regulated by the following norms:

1. The recitation of a third part only of the rosary suffices: but the five decades must be recited continuously.
2. The vocal reiteration must be accompanied by pious meditation on the mysteries.
3. In public recitation the mysteries must be announced in the manner customary in the place; for private recitation, however, it suffices if the vocal recitation is accompanied by meditation on the mysteries.
4. For those belonging to the Oriental rites, amongst whom this devotion is not practiced, the Patriarchs can determine some other prayers in honor of the Blessed Virgin Mary (for those of the Byzantine rite, for example, the Hymn "Akathistos" or the Office "Paraclisis"); to the prayers thus determined are accorded the same indulgences as for the rosary.

Summary of Indulgences

The following historical listing of indulgences for Confraternity members (part I) and the faithful in general (part II) was collected by William R. Lawler —

Granted by the Roman Pontiffs to the Members of the Confraternity of the Most Holy Rosary and to the Faithful in General

Part I
Indulgences Granted to Members Only
I. On the Day of Admission
1. *Plenary* — Confession, Communion, reception into the Confraternity.
2. *Plenary* — After being lawfully inscribed, Confession, Communion in the church or chapel of the Confraternity, recitation of five decades, prayers for the Pope's intention.

II. For Saying the Rosary
A. During the Year
3. *Plenary* — Once a day, for saying entire rosary of fifteen decades, dividing the decades at will, for the triumph of the Holy Mother Church, on condition of Confession, Communion and a visit to a church or public oratory.
4. *Plenary* — Once during life, for the weekly recitation of the entire rosary as is required of members.
5. *10 years*, once a day, for those reciting five decades or a third part of the rosary in the chapel of the rosary, or in any part of the church where the rosary altar can be seen. Members who do not live in a place where the Confraternity is erected may gain this indulgence in any church or public oratory.
6. *10 years and 10 quarantines*, for each recital of the

rosary when said three times a week.

7. *7 years and 7 quarantines*, once a week, for saying the entire rosary.

8. *5 years and 5 quarantines* (i.e., 2025 days), for devoutly saying the Holy Name of Jesus in each Hail Mary.

9. *2 years*, on each of the three days chosen for the weekly obligation, provided the entire rosary is said within the week.

10. *300 days*, for saying five decades.

11. *100 days*, for inducing others to say five decades.

12. *300 days*, once a day, for assisting on Sundays or feast days in a Dominican church, when the rosary is said or sung processionally before carved or painted representations of each Mystery.

B. On Certain Days and Feasts

13. *Plenary* — On the feast of the Annunciation. Confession, Communion and the recitation of the rosary.

14. *10 years and 10 quarantines*, on the feasts of the Purification, Assumption and Nativity of the Blessed Virgin Mary, for recitation of the rosary.

15. *10 years and 10 quarantines*, on the feasts of the Resurrection, and of the Annunciation and Assumption of the Blessed Virgin, when five decades are recited.

16. *7 years and 7 quarantines*, on the other feasts of Our Lord and the Blessed Virgin on which Mysteries of the rosary are celebrated, namely: Visitation of the Blessed Virgin, Christmas, Purification, Compassion of the Blessed Virgin (Friday after Passion Sunday), Ascension, Pentecost and All Saints, for saying at least five decades.

17. *7 years and 7 quarantines*, on Christmas, the Annunciation, Assumption, Nativity of the Blessed

Virgin, for the required weekly recitation of the entire rosary.

18. *100 days*, on the Purification, Annunciation, Visitation, Assumption, Nativity of the Blessed Virgin.

III. For Assisting at the Procession of the Rosary

19. *Plenary* — Confession, Communion, assisting at the procession on the first Sunday of the month, prayers for the intention of the Holy Father, and visiting the chapel of the rosary.

20. *Plenary* — For assisting at a procession (a) on these feasts of the Blessed Virgin: Purification, Annunciation, Visitation, Assumption, Nativity, Presentation, Immaculate Conception, or (b) on any day within their octaves.

21. *5 years*, for maidens who receive a marriage-portion from the alms of the Confraternity and assist at the procession.

22. *100 days*, for taking part in the processions named above.

23. *60 days*, for assisting at the usual rosary procession, or at any carried out with permission of the Ordinary, or when Viaticum is carried to the sick publicly.

IV. For Visiting the Chapel or Church of the Confraternity

24. *Plenary* — First Sunday of the month, on condition of Confession, Communion, visit with prayers for the Pope's intention.

25. *Plenary* — First Sunday of the month. Confession, Communion, prayers before the Blessed Sacrament exposed in the church of the Confraternity, and prayers for the intention of the Holy Father.

26. *Plenary* — Visit to the rosary chapel or church of the Confraternity, Confession, Communion, prayers for the intention of the Holy Father, between midday of the vigil and midnight of the feasts of Christmas,

Epiphany, Resurrection, Ascension, Pentecost, All Saints; once within the octave of All Souls; on any two Fridays of Lent.

27. *Plenary* — On the same conditions, from midday of the vigil to midnight of the following feasts of the Blessed Virgin: Immaculate Conception, Nativity, Presentation, Annunciation, Visitation, Purification, Assumption and Compassion (Friday after Passion Sunday).

28. *Plenary* — On the Sunday in the octave of the Nativity of the Blessed Virgin.

29. *Plenary* — On the third Sunday in April, from Saturday noon to midnight Sunday.

30. *7 years and 7 quarantines*, Confession, Communion, visit to rosary chapel or altar, prayers for the Pope's intention, on Christmas, Easter, Pentecost, Immaculate Conception, Nativity of the Blessed Virgin, Annunciation, Visitation, Assumption, All Saints.

31. *100 days*, once a day, for those who visit the chapel or the altar of the rosary and there pray for the intention of the Holy Father.

V. For Visiting Five Altars

32. Members of the Rosary Confraternity who visit five altars in any church or public oratory (or five times one or two altars where there are not five) on the appointed days noted in the Missal, can gain the same indulgences as if visiting the Station Churches in Rome.

VI. For Saying or Hearing the Votive Mass of the Rosary

33. All indulgences granted for saying the entire Rosary can be gained by priest members of the Confraternity who say the Votive Mass of the Blessed Virgin Mary according to the Roman Missal "pro diversitate temporis," at the Rosary altar (which Votive Mass may be said twice a week); other members who assist

at the Mass can gain the same indulgences provided they say some extra prayers.

34. Those who are in the habit of celebrating or hearing this Mass gain, once a month, all indulgences granted for the usual procession on the first Sunday of the month. Confession and Communion are required.

35. *1 year*, on Saturdays in Lent, for assisting at this Mass and at a sermon on the Blessed Virgin and saying the "Hail, Holy Queen."

VII. For the Devotion of the Fifteen Saturdays

36. *Plenary* — On any three of fifteen consecutive Saturdays. Confession, Communion, visit to a church of the Confraternity with prayers for the Pope's intention.

37. *7 years and 7 quarantines*, on the remaining twelve Saturdays.

VIII. For Devotions During October

38. *Plenary* — On a day of one's choice, for assisting at least ten times at these devotions in a Dominican church. Confession, Communion and prayers for the Pope's intentions are required.

39. *7 years and 7 quarantines*, each time these devotions are attended in a Dominican church.

IX. For Assisting at the Singing of the "Salve Regina"

40. *3 years and 3 quarantines*, for assisting with lighted candles (if it is the custom, otherwise add one Hail Mary), at the singing of the "Salve Regina" on feasts of the Blessed Virgin Mary which are celebrated by the Universal Church, on the principal feasts of the Apostles and on the feasts of the Saints of the Dominican Order in a church of the Confraternity.

41. *100 days*, on every day of the year, if a member of the Confraternity assists daily at the singing of this Antiphon after Compline.

42. *40 days*, on all Saturdays and feast days of the year.

X. For Mental Prayer or Other Spiritual Exercises

43. *Plenary* — Once a month, on a day of one's choice, for meditating daily a half-hour or at least a quarter-hour. Confession and Communion are required.

44. *Plenary* — On any day of the year, for having spent forty days in prayer, mortification and other good works, in memory of the forty days Our Lord passed in the desert. This indulgence may be gained only once in the year, and this on a day of one's choice.

45. *7 years and 7 quarantines*, for every half-hour of mental prayer.

46. *100 days*, for every quarter-hour spent in mental prayer.

XI. For Visiting Sick Members

47. *3 years and 3 quarantines*, for each visit to a sick member of the Confraternity.

48. *100 days*, for exhorting sick members of the Confraternity to receive the Sacraments.

XII. For Praying for Deceased Members

49. *Plenary* — For assisting at the Office of the Dead, which is said in the Dominican churches on the four Anniversaries of the Dead (the third day following the feast of the Purification; July 12; the day following the octave of the feast of St. Augustine; November 10). Confession, Communion and prayers for the Pope's intention are required.

50. *8 years*, for assisting at the funeral services and at the procession for the dead on Saturday, or once a month, in a church of the Confraternity.

51. *3 years and 3 quarantines*, for each attendance at funeral services of a member.

52. *100 days*, for assisting with the Confraternity Cross at the funeral or the anniversaries of members and praying for the intention of the Holy Father.

XIII. For Any Pious Work
>   53.   *60 days*, for any work of charity or piety.

XIV. Indulgences Granted to Members of the Rosary Confraternity at the Hour of Death
>   54.   *Plenary* — Can be imparted to members, even outside Confession, by a priest using the prescribed formula, provided that they have recited the entire Rosary weekly.
>   55.   *Plenary*—Granted those who have recited the entire Rosary at least once in their lives, on condition that they have in their hand a blessed candle of the Rosary while departing from this life.
>   56.   *Plenary* — Granted to those who have received the Sacraments of Penance and Holy Eucharist.
>   57.   *Plenary* — Granted to those who with contrite hearts invoke the Name of Jesus, at least in their heart if they cannot do so with their lips.
>   58.   *Plenary* — Granted to those who, having received the Sacraments of the Church, make profession of faith in the Roman Catholic Church, recite the "Hail, Holy Queen" and commend themselves to the Blessed Virgin.

XV. Indulgences Granted to Deceased Members of the Confraternity
>   59.   In churches of the Dominicans the Rosary altar is privileged for priests of the Order in behalf of a deceased member of the Confraternity.
>   60.   In churches of the Confraternity the Rosary altar is privileged for priests who are members of the Confraternity not only in behalf of a deceased member but in behalf of anyone dead, even though there is another privileged altar in the church. But if there is no other privileged altar, then the Rosary altar is privileged for all priests, even though they are not members of the Confraternity, and in behalf of anyone dead.

Part II

Indulgences that Can Be Gained by Rosarians and the Faithful in General

61. *7 years and 7 quarantines*, on the first Sunday of the month by being present at the Rosary procession.

62. *Plenary*— In memory of the victory gained over the Turks near the Echinades Islands through the aid of the Rosary, a plenary indulgence can be gained for each visit made to the Rosary chapel (or to the image of the Blessed Virgin placed in the church for veneration — S. C. Ind., January 25, 1866), from noon of the day preceding the feast of the Most Holy Rosary until midnight of the feast itself, by all who, having approached the Sacraments, say for the intention of the Holy Father six Our Fathers, six Hail Marys and six Glorys at each visit.

63. *Plenary* — On any day selected within the octave of the feast of the Most Holy Rosary, by all who visit the Rosary chapel or the statue of the Blessed Virgin placed in the church and who during the visit pray for the intention of the Sovereign Pontiff.

64. *Plenary* — Under the same conditions, on the feast of Corpus Christi and on the feast of the titular saint of the church.

65. All and each of the indulgences granted in the above list may be applied to the souls of the faithful departed who are united to God by the bond of charity, except, however, the plenary indulgence at the hour of death.

A Summary of Indulgences Granted to All the Faithful for Devotion to the Rosary

66. *Plenary*—Every time five decades are recited before the Blessed Sacrament either exposed or concealed in the tabernacle. Confession and Communion are necessary conditions.

67. *Plenary* — Once a year, for saying five decades of the Rosary daily while using beads with the Dominican blessing. Confession and communion are necessary conditions.

68. *100 days*, for each Our Father and Hail Mary when saying the entire Rosary or at least five decades on beads with the Dominican blessing.

69. *5 years*, for every five decades.

70. *10 years*, once a day, for saying five decades with others, either privately or publicly.

71. *Plenary* — On the last Sunday of the month, for five decades said three times each week with others; provided that, having gone to Confession and received Communion, one visits a church or public oratory and prays for the intentions of the Holy Father.

72. *Plenary* — On any one of fifteen consecutive Saturdays, for five decades, or other devotions to the Rosary Mysteries. Confession, Communion and a visit to a church or public oratory on each Saturday are required.

73. *Plenary* — For any devout novena in honor of Our Lady of the Rosary. Confession, Communion, visit to a church or public oratory and prayers for the Pope's intentions are required.

74. *5 years*, once on each day of the above novena.

75. *Plenary* — On the feast of the Most Holy Rosary, or on any day within the octave, provided five decades are said on the feast and on each day of the octave,

either privately or publicly. Confession, Communion and a visit to a church or public oratory are required.

76. *Plenary* — For five decades said ten times in October, either publicly or privately, after the octave of the feast of the Most Holy Rosary. Confession, Communion and a visit to a church or public oratory are required.

77. *7 years*, every day in October, for five decades said either publicly or privately.

78. *300 days*, for reciting, "Queen of the Most Holy Rosary, Pray for Us."

79. All these Rosary indulgences may be applied to the souls in Purgatory.

Sources of the Indulgences

1. Gregory XIII, *Gloriosi*, July 15, 1579.
2. St. Pius V, *Consueverunt*, September 17, 1569.
3. Pius X, June 12, 1907.
4. Innocent VIII, October 15, 1484.
5. Changed from 50 years to 10, by Pius XI, May 27, 1935.
6. Leo X, *Pastoris Aeterni*, October 6, 1520.
7. St. Pius V, *Consueverunt*, September 17, 1569.
8. Pius IX, Deer. S. C. Indulg., April 14, 1856.
9. Clement VII, *Etsi Temporalium*, May 8, 1534.
10. Leo XIII, August 29, 1899.
11. Leo XIII, August 29, 1899.
12. S. C. Indulg., May 21, 1892.
13. St. Pius V, *Injunctum Nobis*, June 14, 1566.
14. St. Pius V, *Injunctum Nobis*, June 14, 1566.
15. St. Pius V, *Consueverunt*, September 17, 1569.
16. St. Pius V, *Consueverunt*, September 17, 1569.
17. Sixtus IV, *Pastoris Aeterni*, May 30, 1478; Leo X, *Pastoris Aeterni*, October 6, 1520.
18. Leo X, *Pastoris Aeterni*, October 6, 1520.
19. Gregory XIII, *Ad Augendam*, October 24, 1577.

20. (a) Pius VI, *Dum Praeclara*, February 28, 1561.
    (b) S. C. Indulg., February 25, 1848.
21. Gregory XIII, *Desiderantes*, March 22, 1580.
22. Gregory XIII, *Com Sicut*, January 3, 1579.
23. Gregory XIII, *Gloriosi*, July 15, 1579.
24. Gregory XIII, *Ad Augendam*, March 12, 1577.
25. Gregory XIII, *Ad Augendam*, December 17, 1833.
26. Gregory XIII, *Pastoris Aeterni*, May 5, 1582:
    Gregory XVI, *Ad Augendam*, December 17, 1833: S. C. Indulg., May 12, 1851.
27. Gregory XIII, *Pastoris Aeterni*, May 5, 1582; Clement VIII, *De Salute*, January 18, 1593: Gregory XVI, *Ad Augendam*, December 17, 1833.
28. Clement VIII, *Ineffabilia*, February 12, 1598.
29. Gregory XIII, *Cum Sicut*, January 3, 1579.
30. Clement VIII, *Salvatoris*, January 13, 1593: *De Salute*, January 18, 1593.
31. Gregory XIII, *Cum Sicut*, January 3, 1579.
32. Leo X, May 22, 1518.
33. Leo XIII, *Ubi Primum*, XV, October 2, 1898.
34. Clement X, *Coelestium Munerum*, February 16, 1671.
35. Gregory XIII, *Desiderantes*, March 22, 1580.
36. S. C. Indulg., December 12, 1849.
37. S. C. Indulg., December 12, 1849.
38. S. C. Indulg., August 31, 1885.
39. S. C. Indulg., August 31, 1885.
40. (a) S. C. Indulg., September 18, 1862, *ad 4*.
    (b) Clement VIII, *Ineffabilia*, February 12, 1598.
41. Clement VIII, *Ineffabilia*, February 12, 1598.
42. Leo X, *Pastoris Aeterni*, October 6, 1520.
43. Clement X, *Ad Ea*, January 28, 1671.
44. Pius VII, *Ad Augendam*, February 16, 1808.
45. Clement X., *Ad Ea*, January 28, 1671.
46. Clement X., *Ad Ea*, January 28, 1671.
47. Clement VIII, *Ineffabilia*, February 12, 1598.
48. Gregory XIII, *Cum Sicut*, January 3, 1579.
49. Pius VII, *Ad Augendam*, February 16, 1808.

50. Gregory XIII, *Desiderantes*, March 22, 1580.
51. Clement VIII, *Ineffabilia*, February 12, 1598.
52. Gregory XIII, *Cum Sicut*, January 3, 1579.
53. Gregory XIII, *Gloriosi*, July 15, 1579.
54. Innocent VIII, October 13, 1483; S. C. Indulg., August 10, 1899.
55. Adrian VI, *Illius Qui*, April 1, 1523.
56. St. Pius V, *Consueverunt*, September 17, 1569.
57. Leo XIII, Rescr. S. C. Indulg., August 19, 1899.
58. Clement VIII, *Ineffabilia*, February 12, 1598.
59. Gregory XIII, *Omnium Saluti*, September 1, 1582.
60. S. C. Indulg., *Cameracen*, June 7, 1842; Pius IX, *Omnium Saluti*, March 3, 1857.
61. St. Pius V, *Consueverunt*, September 17, 1569.
62. St. Pius V, *Salvatoris*, March 5, 1572: S. C. Indulg., January 25, 1866, and April 5, 1869: July 7, 1885.
63. Benedict XIII, *Pretiosus*, May 26, 1727: S. C. Indulg., July 7, 1885.
64. Gregory XIII, *Desiderantes*, March 22, 1580.
65. Innocent XI, *Ad Ea*, June 15, 1679.
66. Pius XI, *Ad Sancti Dominici*, September 4, 1927. See *Preces et Pia Opera*, No. 360.
67. See *Preces et Pia Opera*, No. 360.
68. The same as 67.
69. Sixtus IV, May 12, 1479: S. C. Indulg., August 29, 1899: S. Paen. Ap., March 18, 1932. See *Preces et Pia Opera*, No. 360.
70. S. C. Indulg., May 12, 1857 and August 29, 1899: S. Paen. Ap., March 18, 1932. See *Preces et Pia Opera*, No. 360.
71. S. C. Indulg., May 12, 1857 and August 29, 1899: S. Paen. Ap., March 18, 1932. See *Preces et Pia Opera*, No. 360.
72. S. C. Indulg., September 21, 1889 and September 17, 1892; S. Paen. Ap., August 3, 1936. See *Preces et Pia Opera*, No. 360.
73. Pius IX, January 3, 1849: S. C. Episc. et Regul., January 28, 1850; S. C. Indulg., November 26, 1876: S. Paen. Ap., June 29, 1932. See *Preces et Pia Opera*, No. 361.
74. Same as 73.
75. *Preces et Pia Opera*, No. 363.

76. Same as 75.
77. S. C. Indulg., July 23, 1898 and August 29, 1899: S. Paen. Ap., March 18, 1932. See *Preces et Pia Opera*, No. 363.
78. S. C. 5. Off., October 1, 1915; 5. Paen. Ap., November 24, 1933. See *Preces et Pia Opera*, No. 359.
79. Canon 930 (1917 version).

This collection is found in *The Rosary of Mary*, edited by William Raymond Lawler. Paterson, New Jersey: St. Anthony Guild Press, 1944. Used with permission.

Bibliography

Auchinleck Manuscript, "A Penni Worth of Witte: Florice and Blanchflour and other Pieces of English Poetry from the Auchinleck Manuscript," ed. David Laing. Edinburgh: The Abbotsford Club, 1857.

Ahmad, Khurshid, ed. *Islam: Its Meaning and Message.* London: Islamic Council of Europe, 1976.

Arnold, Jeanne. *A Man of Faith.* Hollywood, California: Family Theater, Inc., 1983.

Barclay, Florence L. *The Rosary.* New York: G. P. Putnam's Sons, 1910.

Béchaux, Henri. "*Les Mysteres du Rosaire,*" *La Vie Spirituelle* 98 (1958), pp. 215-24.

Beissel, Stephen. *Geschichte der Verehrung Marias in Deutschland Wahrend des Mittelalters*, vol. 1. Freiburg: Herder, 1909.

Benedictine Monks of Solesmes, ed. *Papal Teachings—The Holy Rosary*, trans. Paul J. Oligny, O.F.M. Boston: Daughters of St. Paul, 1980.

Blackman, Winifred S. "Rosaries," *Encyclopedia of Religion and Ethics* 10: pp. 847-56, ed. James Hastings. New York: Charles Scribners, 1919.

Broomhall, Marshall. *Islam in China*. London: Morgan & Scott, LTD, 1910.

Buche, John. "Instructions for the Use of the Beads 1589," *English Recusant Literature 1588-1640*, vol. 77, ed. D. M. Rogers. Menston, England: Scholar Press, 1971.

Camacho, H. M. "De Montfort and the Rosary," *Our Lady's Digest* 19 (1959): pp. 329-31.

Canice, Father, OFM Cap. "The Rosary," *Irish Ecclesiastical Record* 82 (1954): pp. 217-25.

Carpenter, H. "The Rosary: Its Doctrinal Base," *Cross and Crown* 20 (1968): pp. 298-300.

Casanowicz, Immanuel M. "The Collection of Rosaries in the United States National Museum," *Proceedings of the U.S. National Museum*, no. 1667 (1909).

Devas, R. P. "The Rosary Tradition Defined and Defended," *American Catholic Quarterly Review* 41 (1916): pp. 128-47.

Davis, H. H. "A Rosary Confraternity Charter of 1579 and the Cardinal of Santa Susanna," *Catholic Historical Review* 48 (1962): pp. 321-42.

De Marchi, John. *The Story of Fatima*. Republished at Billings, Montana: The Mother of Christ Crusade, 1947.

De Montfort, St. Louis. *The Secret of the Rosary*, trans. Mary Barbour, T.O.P. Bayshore, New York: Montfort Publications, 1976.

Del Prado, Norberto, O.P. *Ensenanzas del Rosario*. Vergara: El Santismo Rosario, 1913.

Doerr, Othmar. "The Our Father and Hail Mary in the Baumberg Hermit's Rule," *Das Institut der Inclusen in Suddeutschland*. Munster: Herder, 1934.

Doheny, William and Joseph P. Kelly. *Papal Documents on Mary*. Milwaukee: The Bruce Publishing Company, 1954.

Dollen, C. "The Rosary: A School of Theology," *Our Lady's Digest* 19 (1965): pp. 259-61.

Dos Santos, Lucia. *Lucia Speaks — Memoirs and Letters of Sister Lucia*, trans. Dominican Nuns of the Perpetual Rosary.

Washington, New Jersey: AMI Press, 1976.

Erzbischofliches Diozesan—Museum Koln. *500 Jahre Rosenkranz 1475 Koln 1975.* Cologne: J. P. Bachem, 1975.

Esser, Thomas. *Geschichte des Englischen Grusses in Historisches Jahrbuch der Gorres-Gesellschaft.* Basel: Herder, 1884.

Finley, Mitchell B. "Recovering the Rosary," *America* 148 (1983): p. 351.

Flanagan, Donal. "The Rosary," *Furrow* 21 (1970): pp. 264-66.

Fuerst, Anthony N. *This Rosary.* Milwaukee: The Bruce Publishing Company, 1942.

Galvin, J. J. "Our Rosary Beads," *American Ecclesiastical Review* 125 (1951): pp. 280-83.

Garrigou-Lagrange, Reginald. "The Meaning of the Rosary," *Doctrine and Life* (October-November 1952): pp. 227-33.

Gasquet, F. A. "An English Rosary Book of the Fifteenth Century," *The Downside Review* (December 1893).

Goldhizer, Ignaz. "De L'Ascetisme Aux Premiers Temps de L'Islam," *Revue de l'Histoire des Religions* 37 (1898): pp. 314-24.

————. "Le Rosaire dans L'Islam," *Revue de l'Histoire des Religions* 21 (1890): pp. 295-300.

Gribble, Richard. "Roses of October," *Queen of All Hearts* (November-December 1986), pp. 18-19.

"How the Chinese Pray the Rosary," *Catholic Digest* 18 (May 1954): pp. 100-105.

Ihm, Claudia C., ed. *The Papal Encyclopedia*, vols. 2, 3, 4, 5. Raleigh, North Carolina: McGrath Publishing Company, 1981.

Jarrett, Bede. *The Life of Dominic.* Westminster, Maryland: The Newman Bookshop, 1947.

John Paul II, Pope. "*Familiaris Consortio*," encyclical letter of November 22, 1981, in *More Postconciliar Documents*, ed. Austin Flannery, O.P., pp. 815-98. Grand Rapids, Michigan: William B. Eerdmans Publishing Company, 1982.

Kelly, Frederick. "Prayer Beads in World Religions: The Rosary," *Worldmission* 31 (Spring 1980): pp. 20-25.

Kirsch, Winfried. *Handbuch des Rosenkranzes*. Vienna: DomVerlag, 1950.

Klein, F. A. *The Religion of Islam*. London: Curzon Press, 1971.

Klinkhammer, Karl J. *Adolf van Essen und Seine Werke Der Rosenkranz in der Geschichtlichen Situation Seiner Entstehung und in Seinem Bleibenden Angliegen*. Frankfurt: Josef Knecht, 1972.

Lane, E. W. *Manners and Customs of Modern Egyptians*. London: Dent Publishing Company, 1908.

Langdon, H. "The Rosary: Dated or Dateless," *Liguorian* 67 (1979): pp. 34-36.

Lawler, William Raymond, ed. *The Rosary of Mary*. Paterson, New Jersey: St. Anthony Guild Press, 1944.

Lawrence, Claude, OMI. "The Rosary From the Beginning to Our Day" *Christ to the World* 28 (1983): pp. 194-201.

Leo XIII, Pope. *Supremi Apostolatus*, September 1, 1883; *Octobri mense*, September 22, 1891; *Magnae Dei Matris*, September 7, 1892: *Laetitae sanctae*, September 8, 1893: *Iucunda semper*, September 8, 1894; *Adiutricem populi*, September 5, 1895: *Fidentem piumque*, September 20, 1897; *Augustissimae Virginis*, September 12, 1897. Encyclical letters.

Lescher, Wilfrid. *St. Dominic and the Rosary*. London: Washbourne Publishers, 1902.

McNicholas, John T. "The Rosary," *The Ecclesiastical Review* (October, 1917).

McGuire, E. A. "Old Irish Rosaries: Plates," *Furrow* 5 (1954): pp. 97-105.

Masson, R. "L'Histoire du Rosaire," *Marie* 11 (1958): pp. 463-65.

Monier-Williams, Sir Monier. *Hinduism*. London: Society for Promoting Christian Knowledge, 1878.

_____. *Brahmanism and Hinduism*. London: John Murray, Albemarle St., 1891.

O'Connor, D. *"The Rosary for Today's Catholics*," Our Lady's Digest 19 (1964): pp. 33-34.

Odell, Catherine M. "The Rosary," *Our Sunday Visitor* 71 (1982): pp. 12-15.

Pennington, Basil, OSCO. "The Rosary: An Ancient Prayer for All of Us," *Our Sunday Visitor* 72 (1983): p. 3.

Peyton, Patrick, CSC. "The Meaning of the Rosary," *Catholic Layman* 79 (1965): pp. 26-28.

_____. *All for Her*. Hollywood: Family Theater Publications, 1973.

Pius V, Pope St. *Salvatoris Domini*, encyclical letter, March 5, 1572, in *The Holy Rosary — Papal Teachings*, trans. Paul J. Oligny, OFM. Boston: Daughters of St. Paul, 1980.

Roberts, John R. "The Rosary in Elizabethan England," *The Month* 32, 218 (1964): pp. 192-197.

"Saint Joseph and the Rosary in Art," *Dominicana* 42 (1957): pp. 5-6.

Scherschel, Rainer. *Das Rosenkranz das Jesusgebet des Westons*. Basel: Herder, 1979.

Schmitz, Wilhelm. *Das Rosenkranzgebet im 15 und am Angang des 16 Jahrhunderts*. Freiburg: Herder, 1903.

Shaughnessy, Patrick. "Rosaries: Twenty-One Different Kinds," *Priest* 9 (1953): pp. 770-73.

Shaw, J. G. *The Story of the Rosary*. Milwaukee: The Bruce Publishing Company, 1954.

Shea, G. "The Rosary: Its Nature and Excellence," *Our Lady's Digest* 18 (1963): pp. 160-82.

Stevens, C. "The Rosary: Instrument of Renewal," *Our Sunday Visitor* 64 (1975): p. 1.

Snow, R. J. "Salve Regina," *New Catholic Encyclopedia* 12: p. 1002. New York: McGraw-Hill Book Company, 1967.

Tansey, A. "The Secret Rosary of Japan," *Our Sunday Visitor* 61 (1973): p. 1.

Thurston, Herbert, S.J. "Our Popular Devotions II: The Rosary I," *The Month* 96 (1900): pp. 403-18.

_____. "Our Popular Devotions II: The Rosary I, The Rosary

Amongst the Carthusians," *The Month* 96 (1900): pp. 513-27.

_____. "Our Popular Devotions II: The Rosary III," *The Month* 96 (1900): pp. 620-38.

_____. "Our Popular Devotions II: The Rosary IV, Was the Rosary Instituted by St. Dominic?" *The Month* 97 (1901): pp. 67-79.

_____. "Our Popular Devotions II: The Rosary V, The Rebutting Evidence," *The Month* 97 (1901): pp. 172-88.

_____. "Our Popular Devotions II: The Rosary VI, The Rise and Growth of the Dominican Tradition," *The Month*, 97 (1901): pp. 286-304.

_____. "Our Popular Devotions II: The Rosary VII, The Archaeology of the Rosary Beads," *The Month* 97 (1901): pp. 383-404.

_____. "Our Popular Devotions VI: The So-Called Brigettine Rosary," *The Month* 100 (1902): pp. 189-203.

_____. "Alan de Rupe and His Indulgence of 60,000 Years," *The Month* 111 (1902): pp. 281-99.

_____. "The Name of the Rosary," *The Month* 111 (1908): pp. 518-29.

_____. "The Name of the Rosary II," *The Month* 111 (1908): pp. 610-23.

_____. "Notes on Familiar Prayers 1: The Origins of the Hail Mary," *The Month* 121 (1913): pp. 162-76.

_____. "Genuflections and Aves: A Study in Rosary Origins, Part I," *The Month* 127 (1916): pp. 441-51.

_____. "Genuflections and Aves: A Study in Rosary Origins, Part II," *The Month* 127 (1916): pp. 546-559.

_____. "What is the Dominican Tradition of the Rosary?" *The Month* 144 (1924): pp. 330-43.

_____. "The History of the Rosary in All Countries," *Journal of the Society of Arts* (February, 1902), pp. 57-68.

_____. "Hail Mary," *Catholic Encyclopedia* 7:110-12. New York: Robert Appleton Company, 1907.

_____. "Rosary," *Catholic Encyclopedia* 8:184-87. New York: Robert Appleton Company, 1907.

_____. "Apostles Creed," *Catholic Encyclopedia* 1:629-32. New York: Robert Appleton Company, 1907.

Waddell, L. A. *The Buddhism of Tibet*. Cambridge, England: W. Heffer & Sons, Limited, 1934.

Walsh, William T. *Our Lady of Fatima*. Garden City, New York: Image Books, 1954.

Ward, Maisie. *The Splendor of the Rosary*. New York: Sheed & Ward, 1945.

Watkins, Oscar D. *A History of Penance*, vol. 2. New York: Burt Franklin, 1961.

Wilkins, Eithne. *The Rose-Garden Game*. London: Victor Gollancz, LTD, 1969.

_____. "Why We Call it the Rosary," *Catholic Digest* 34 (1970): pp. 65-78.

Willam, Franz M. *The Rosary: Its History and Meaning*, trans. Edwin Kaiser, C.P.P.S. New York: Benziger Brothers, Inc., 1953.

Index

193